T0293252

Management Lessons
from the Great Explorers

Management Lessons from the Great Explorers

Ralph Kliem, PMP, CBCP

CRC Press
Taylor & Francis Group
Boca Raton London New York

CRC Press is an imprint of the
Taylor & Francis Group, an **informa** business

AN AUERBACH BOOK

First Edition published 2022
by CRC Press
6000 Broken Sound Parkway NW, Suite 300, Boca Raton, FL 33487–2742

and by CRC Press
4 Park Square, Milton Park, Abingdon, Oxon, OX14 4RN

© 2022 Taylor & Francis Group, LLC

CRC Press is an imprint of Taylor & Francis Group, LLC

Library of Congress Cataloging-in-Publication Data
A catalog record has been requested for this book

ISBN: 978-1-032-19095-2 (hbk)
ISBN: 978-0-367-46433-2 (pbk)
ISBN: 978-1-003-02873-4 (ebk)

DOI: 10.1201/9781003028734

Typeset in Garamond
by Apex CoVantage, LLC

Contents

Preface

Managing projects is like going on an expedition. You have a sponsor, vision, goal, team, path, and resources. But you also have many challenges. Risks and issues. Morale concerns and people leaving for one reason or another. Change of sponsors. Political interference. Reduced funding. Some happy but also upset stakeholders. The scope may have to change based upon additional information. If that is not enough, if the project fails, you receive the blame, but if it succeeds, you get to manage another project.

After reading about expeditions of historic explorers over the years, the parallels to projects struck me. Also, my experience as a young officer in the US Army both in the frigid areas of northern Alaska where the temperature dropped to minus 50 to 75 degrees Fahrenheit and the hot deserts in the southwest of the United States where the temperatures exceeded 120 degrees only added to my interest in expeditions, not to mention my travels around the globe over the years experiencing oceanic storms, life-threatening disease, earthquakes, and rogue waves.

Hence my long desire to write a book like this one. The stories of the explorers in this book continue to fascinate me to this day. Christopher Columbus, Jacque Cartier, James Cook, Roald Amundsen, Ernest Shackleton: These names are just a few of the men covered in this book whose experiences offer lessons to project managers. Admittedly, the selection of individuals covered is eclectic, but they are the ones who have influenced my thinking and even performance as a project manager over several decades. I also must admit that some of the explorers covered, as to their beliefs and actions, have much to be desired, and I find their character somewhat repugnant. Some were murders and slavers. Some were thieves. From a purely project management perspective, these men have much to offer regarding project management in today's business and public environments. Henry Ford is reputed to have said that history is bunk (not exactly those words), but did say that it had no relevancy to the present. I disagree. Much can be learned from history. I more subscribed to the thinking of George Santayana who said, "Those who cannot remember the past are condemned to repeat it." Winston Churchill wrote something along similar lines: "Those that fail to learn from history are doomed to repeat it." I partially agree, but view these two statements as taking a negative perspective of history. I prefer to view history as a subject that offers positive as well as negative lessons that project managers can leverage in their projects and avoid mistakes.

I want to express my thanks to a good friend, J.R. Hudson. Over the years, he taught me the basics of sailing throughout the Puget Sound and always renews my interest in the subject. I also want to thank my friends, Sean Thomas, author, and his wife, Doris Thomas, who also sparked my interest in fishing the frigid waters of Alaska and who are leaders within the Coast Guard auxiliary.

Ralph Kliem, PMP, CBCP

Chapter 1

George Vancouver: Understanding the Context

Taking a systematic approach that involves collecting and compiling data about an environment, converting the data into information, and distinguishing between what is and is not important.

James Cook is considered by many historians as one of the greatest explorers of England, if not the world. Mention George Vancouver and most exploration enthusiasts would also agree that one other person might be on the same level with Cook: George Vancouver.

Background

George Vancouver was a protégé of Cook's, having served as a midshipman with Cook. In fact, he was there in Hawaii when Cook met his demise at the hands of natives. While on that infamous third voyage, sailing on the HMS *Discovery*, Vancouver came close to death as a young man.

Vancouver learned much from Cook and the crew while in his early teen years. He learned how to run a well-disciplined ship under arduous circumstances. He learned cartography and other navigation skills. He also acquired knowledge and skills related to preparing a vessel for long arduous journeys, such as provisioning to sustain crews on long voyages, understanding the customs of indigent peoples,

DOI: 10.1201/9781003028734-1

traveling through unknown treacherous waters, and adapting to whatever environment he found himself.

In many regards, Vancouver's and Cook's personalities were similar. They both had a bad temper. They focused on the goals, sometimes at great expense to the welfare of the crew. They were strict disciplinarians, though Vancouver may have been a bit harsher. They had their differences with some well-connected subordinates. Toward the end of their great expeditions, they suffered from ailments that affected their judgments. In some respects, too, they were outsiders, Cook being of Scottish descent and Vancouver of Dutch. When Vancouver started his great expeditions in the Pacific, he followed essentially the same route that Cook often followed, circling under the Cape of Good Hope and then sailing east toward New Zealand, Australia, Tahiti, and Hawaii. Both had experienced naval warfare: Cook during the French and Indian Wars in North American and Vancouver at the Battle of the Saints in the Caribbean.

Vancouver and Cook were different, however, in other respects. Unlike Cook, Vancouver came from better social and economic circumstances. His father was a deputy customs collector, considered at the time something equivalent to upper middle class; Cook came from much more humble circumstances. Vancouver started as a midshipman at a young age whereas Cook began as an ordinary seaman at a relatively older age in his late 20s. In the end, Cook died at the hands of Hawaiian natives while Vancouver returned to England to find himself ridiculed, threatened, and ailing.

Vancouver, of course, had the benefit of learning from the experiences of Captain Cook during all the voyages, although he was not a midshipman until after he had been at sea for two years. After those two years, he became a midshipman, supporting other officers by performing responsibilities such as standing watch with officers, updating logs, and assisting crew members working the sails. He also learned the rudiments of navigation, science, and mathematics. He also learned about the importance of maintaining the health of the crew, such as providing antiscorbutic food to help prevent scurvy, cleaning the decks, and washing and drying garments. He would follow these very same practices when he commanded the HMS *Discovery* to the west coast of North America.

Still, Vancouver had some advantages that Cook lacked on his expedition. Cook only had the luxury of a chronometer on his third voyage; Vancouver had the luxury of a chronometer from the start. He was also experienced, following virtually the same route heading to North America. He knew what to expect from the natives, ocean, and land, which also helped him to understand and deal with some of the circumstances that he faced. Still, this knowledge and understanding should not detract from his great accomplishments. He experienced tremendous challenges throughout the Pacific region. In a sense, these challenges were more complex because he had to deal with many more native tribes that Cook was unfamiliar with and wrestle with other European powers, such as Russia and Spain.

Upon returning from Cook's third voyage, Vancouver had served over seven years at sea. He was ready to take the exam to become an officer in the British navy. He passed the exam and became one in 1780.

In 1781, Britain faced a coalition of nations that threatened its dominance of the seas. Austria, Denmark, France, Holland, Prussia, Russia, and Sweden formed a coalition to protect themselves from British interference on the high seas. This situation provided Vancouver with an opportunity to participate in the Royal Navy as an officer, being assigned to the HMS *Martin*, which functioned as a convoy ship between England and Belgium and subsequently sailed to the Caribbean. Vancouver then served as a lieutenant on a vessel called HMS *Fame* on which he commanded a section of a battery and performed supervisory duties on deck. It was during this experience on the HMS *Fame* that he witnessed the ravages of yellow fever and scurvy and the need for preventive measures. Like the military of today, peace can slow an officer's advancement due to a downturn. The same occurred for Vancouver when in 1783 he found himself placed in inactive service and like the others received half pay. In short order, Vancouver found an officer's slot on the HMS *Europa* and once again was on the way to the Caribbean, Jamaica. In Port Royal, he would impress the commodore who would prove instrumental in accelerating his career and would strike a close professional relationship with Joseph Whidbey who helped Vancouver in surveying Kingston Harbor and played a pivotal role in the charting and surveying of the Pacific Northwest.

Situation

In 1783, demobilization returned. Vancouver, however, escaped this one. Through his connections and opportunities afforded to him and thanks to the deaths of more senior lieutenants, Vancouver received the opportunity to serve as a lieutenant, more like an executive officer, on the HMS *Discovery*, which was not the same vessel under Captain Cook. His responsibilities increased dramatically from ensuring that provisions and supplies arrived and were stowed into holds, as well as ensuring rigging, masts, and sails were installed. International tensions arose over who controlled Nootka Sound, and like Captain Henry Roberts, Vancouver and Whidbey were reassigned. Vancouver and Whidbey were both reassigned to a captured French vessel called the HMS *Courageux*. International tensions had subsided at the Nootka Convention, and Vancouver and Whidbey were reassigned back to the HMS *Discovery*, which had been used to impress men into the British navy. Vancouver was assigned as captain of the ship.

The Nootka Convention resulted in a treaty that contained unclear terms of agreement between Britain and Spain. Lands and buildings, seized earlier, would be restored to Britain and reparations paid. The challenge was that no buildings were ever seized by Spain, and the British owned no land. Both parties would be allowed to conduct trade with the natives of the Pacific Northwest. In exchange the

British were not to violate Spanish territories in North America, adding another complexity because the northernmost point of Spanish settlements remained unclear. Because of the diplomatic mess, Vancouver was sent to Nootka Sound and his Spanish counterpart Don Juan Francisco de la Bodega y Quadra.

Vancouver had three goals to achieve. The first one was to conduct a survey of the Pacific Northwest coast of North America; the second was to meet with Don Juan Francisco de la Bodega y Quadra (often referred to as Quadra), the commandant at Nootka Sound of the future Vancouver Island, to conduct cessions to the British; and the third was to prove or disprove whether the waterway, famously known as the Northwest Passage, existed. Vancouver had accomplished all three goals but to a large extent because of his ability to adapt to a tough set of circumstances. He would accomplish these three goals with two vessels, the HMS *Discovery* (commanded by Vancouver) and the HMS *Chatman* (commanded by Lt. William Broughton), two vessels for exploring the Pacific Northwest.

Expedition

The expedition began on April 1, 1792, departing from Falmouth, England. As mentioned earlier, he took the route that included the places explored initially by Captain Cook. He stopped at the Canary Islands for provisions, which entailed at one point being thrown in the water by Spanish soldiers while he attempted to defend his crew in what appeared to be a brawl. (One would think that such an incident would entail harboring resentment toward the Spanish, but the incident did not affect him in his later dealings with them as the reader will see later.) From there, the vessels proceeded toward Australia, Van Dieman's Land (Tasmania today), New Zealand, Tahiti, and Sandwich Islands (the Hawaiian Islands today); along the Pacific Northwest (via the coast of California and what would later be known as Oregon and Washington state); and arriving, ultimately, at Nootka Sound. One significant result of the journey was passing through the Strait of Juan de Fuca and taking possession of it for the British.

Before meeting with Quadra, however, Vancouver conducted an extensive exploration. He spotted two Spanish vessels in the harbor, which reputedly took him by surprise. It was after that point that he conducted extensive explorations of Puget Sound and Vancouver Island. A significant event was that he had met with Robert Gray, the American discoverer of the Columbia River. The crew performed extensive exploration of the Puget Sound and had named several sites, too. These included Mt. Rainier, Mt. Hood, Hood Canal, and Puget Sound. He also conducted an extensive survey of Vancouver Island before meeting with Quadra.

Despite lacking concrete diplomatic instructions, he was able to build a cordial relationship with Quadra. Vancouver seemed to have put his negative incident in the Canaries aside as he and Quadra established and maintained a positive relationship. Quadra was also a hospitable host despite having instructions that were inadequate. The relationship between the two men was remarkable, considering their countries almost came to the brink of war, as well as being military competitors and culturally different. Vancouver adapted to the challenge as much as Quadra. The relationship between the two became so positive that the two parties agreed to name, called Vancouver Island today, Quadra and Vancouver Island.

The strength of the relationship between Vancouver and Quadra was further demonstrated when the former stopped in Monterey, California, on the way to the Sandwich Islands. Quadra demonstrated hospitality by allowing the HMS *Discovery* and HMS *Chatham* to make repairs, providing provisions, and helping to pursue deserters from the later vessel and another one called the HMS *Daedalus*. The HMS *Daedalus* had originally arrived in Nootka Sound, served as a supply ship to the HMS *Discovery* and HMS *Chatham*, and had the same responsibility in Monterey.

During his explorations of the Pacific Northwest, Vancouver faced difficulty using the HMS *Discovery* and the HMS *Chatham* to conduct a detailed exploration of the coastlines, which were rocky mountainsides steep along treacherous waters and amid rain and fog. He had no alternative but to employ small boats to conduct most of the surveys. Conducting surveys in the small boats proved a hardship as crew members, especially the officers, including Vancouver himself, conducted surveys. This hardship caused considerable disgruntlement among officers and crew, but he managed to complete their surveys and charting.

While he often had a good relationship with people outside of his command, Vancouver did face some challenges with his crew, thanks largely to his personality. He was often aloof with his officers and crew, and when he did engage with them, he did so in an irritable and tempest manner, which increased upon the return voyage to England. He was also unrelenting in achieving the goals of his expedition while having a limited desire to receive feedback. He was known not to spare the lash if a crew member failed to comply with his directives. At one point, he disciplined a relative of Prime Minister William Pitt, which eventually helped to sink Vancouver's career; the incident became known as the Camelford Incident.

Vancouver faced challenges from traders both in Hawaii and Nootka Sound. Their behavior often presented some complications. Traders often abused Hawaiian women. In one instance, he returned two young Hawaiian women to the Sandwich Islands after they were abducted and taken to Nootka Sound. In fact, the Hawaiians had become so irritated and angry at the traders, they had abducted two of them, who remained "hostages" of King Kamehameha to prevent additional abuses but, interestingly, became chiefs and advisers to the king.

Vancouver returned to England in September 1795, without much fanfare, after traveling more than 74,000 miles, which was more mileage than Captain Cook. He was publicly maligned, threatened, and assaulted, eventually dying from health complications at the age of 40.

Lessons

So, what are some of the key lessons (Figure 1.1) project managers learn from George Vancouver's experience in understanding the context?

Use the knowledge and experience of others to understand the context. Knowledge and experience are a powerful combination when charting unknown territory. Vancouver had the benefit of both. He gained substantial understanding of how to deal with people from different cultures, such as the Tahitians and the Hawaiians. He attributed the need for understanding and assessing different cultures. Like Cook, Vancouver failed sometimes to deal with indigenous people, such as once in Nootka Sound when he did not allow a tribal chief, named Maquinna, to board the HMS *Discovery*, failing to realize the native was of high stature. However, Vancouver realized his mistake and, along with Quadra, made amends to the native chief. Vancouver also built good relationships with the Hawaiians, especially with King Kamehameha, even to the point of trying to reduce conflict among chiefs and improving their self-governance as an island nation.

Accept the fact that not all data and information will be readily available. Sometimes all the data and information are unavailable. Under such circumstances contextual, understanding is difficult. Especially having to decide something important. Vancouver and Quadra had to implement the treaties of the Nootka Convention. Some provisions of the treaties were unclear and not applicable, such as restoring buildings and land to the British when none existed, and the boundaries of the northern Spanish territories of the Pacific Northwest were vague. Nevertheless, Vancouver made some decisions, negotiated options with Quadra, and sent Lt. Broughton of the HMS *Chatham* to obtain further instructions from London.

Be flexible when contextual understanding is difficult. Rigidity in thought can prove disastrous. Vancouver receives mixed reviews regarding this lesson. When heading to Nootka Sound and exploring the Pacific Northwest, he realized that the treacherous coastline did not lend itself to using the HMS *Discovery* or the HMS *Chatham* to survey the coastlines. Instead, despite the hardship to himself, his officers, and the crew, he used small boats. At one point, this realization manifested itself when both the HMS *Discovery* and the HMS *Chatham* were grounded on

The Lessons of George Vancouver

- Use the knowledge and experience of others to understand the context
- Accept the fact that not all data and information will be readily available
- Be flexible when contextual understanding is difficult
- Maintain good cordial relationships with important stakeholders in the environment

Figure 1.1 The Lessons of George Vancouver.

rocks in Queen Charlotte Strait. Once the vessels became free, the surveys continued despite the fact that many of the officers and crew were jaded. His inflexibility often caused severe morale problems. Yet, over a four-year period, he lost few men to disease due to insistence on complying with rigorous health standards, even to the point of administering harsh discipline. He had limited focus regarding factors like morale impacting performance.

His focus on his goals for the expedition impaired his ability to understand the context of his environment, resulting in overlooking some significant opportunities for discovery. For example, he failed to discover some of the major rivers of the Pacific Northwest, such as the Columbia, Skeena, Fraser, and Stikine because he concentrated on the coastlines and on finding the Strait of Juan de Fuca. However, he did converse with the American explorer, Robert Gray, who had discovered the mouth of the Columbia River. Vancouver had passed by the mouth of the great river; he later assigned Lt. Broughton to explore it, covering about 100 miles inland.

Maintain good cordial relationships with important stakeholders in the environment. Vancouver, despite not being a diplomat, performed this role well, and it provided immense benefits to the expedition. He not only helped to resolve problems over traders with the Hawaiians and helped in the cession of Hawaii, which failed, to England. He also maintained a positive dialogue with Quadra who shared information about Gray's discovery of Columbia, as well as provided provisions and support when the HMS *Discovery* and HMS *Chatman* arrived at Monterey, California. These cordial relations, despite the pomp and ceremony of King Kamehameha when greeting him and the lavish cordiality of Quadra, did not tarnish his judgment. He resisted the temptation to give the Hawaiians arms, and he was willing to respond to the behavior of natives, resulting in problems, such as thefts in Tahiti and Hawaii. Overall, he maintained cordial relationships, displaying a willingness to learn native language and customs which provided valuable data and information for understanding the context of his environment.

Final Thoughts

Anyone who lives or has visited the Pacific Northwest, whether they realized it, sees his influence. From Seattle in Washington to Vancouver in British Columbia in the north to Hawaii in the south Pacific, his imprint is tremendous. Many of the names he chose reflect members of his crew, as well as many of the sponsors of his expedition. Ironically, much of the expedition's success is due more to his ability to assess his environment despite being given a vague goal of carrying out the terms of the Nootka Convention. In one sense, he was a fitting legacy of Captain James Cook. In another, he left a tremendous legacy to the people of Canada and the United States.

Project managers often suffer the same fate as Vancouver. They receive vague goals that not even the sponsors of their projects understand. A famous example in the field of project management is the project manager tells everyone on his team to start working while he goes and talks to the customer to see what he or she wants.

Chapter 2

Christopher Columbus: Having a Vision

Foreseeing a future state based upon existing knowledge and capabilities and the resulting benefits and sticking to it.

One of the greatest ironies of Christopher Columbus is that his influence is everywhere in the Western Hemisphere, and yet he remains a man of mystery. Just about everything known about him is open to question. No one seems to agree on anything about him other than he crossed the Atlantic in 1492 with *La Pinta*, *La Niña*, and *Santa María*. Controversy surrounds the way he looks; whether he was Jewish or Christian; which side he served on during a naval battle between the Genoese and the Portuguese and French; the year he was born; if he came from a family of wool weavers or had royal blood; whether he corresponded with some of the well-known cartographers of his time, such as Paolo dal Pozzo Toscanelli; and even where his body is buried, let alone where he was born. The only apparent agreement is that he took four trips across the Atlantic based upon a vision that he doggedly believed was correct.

One side of Christopher Columbus is often overlooked: being a visionary. Just about everyone who studies him agrees that he was one hell of a navigator and a supreme expert on seamanship. However, little attention is paid to being a visionary.

Background

Before discussing this visionary genius, it is best to describe what we do know about one of the world's first men of mystery.

DOI: 10.1201/9781003028734-2

Columbus, according to historians and some of his contemporaries, for an uneducated man, was well schooled in the art of navigation and seamanship. Much of his background in both subjects were the result of being self-educated and having extensive experience. From a self-education standpoint, he read widely on geography, history, and natural history and other topics, especially ones related to navigation and seamanship. He also taught himself several languages, including Castilian and Portuguese. Being a religious man of the times, he was knowledge-able of the Bible and, during his expeditions to the New World, had his crew recite Ave Maria during vespers and participate in other religious activities, albeit many historians agree that he did not hold an absolutist position regarding religion. He subscribed to religion because it functioned as a paradigm of the day from which he viewed the world. His religion did not prevent him from increasing his scien-tific knowledge as it related to navigation and seamanship. He was also inquisitive, seeking the knowledge and experience of others if he could not find the answers in contemporary books and charts. Columbus, it is fair to say, was pious but not closed-minded.

Columbus appeared to be somewhat more advanced in his thinking for the times, especially when it related to topics like the natural sciences. Unlike many contemporaries, he had advanced knowledge of the trade winds and was quite skill-ful in mathematics which helped in calculating positions at sea. He did not believe in wild sea creatures lurking below the surface of the oceans waiting to swallow ships like many members of his crew. In fact, Columbus seemed to hold no prejudices when it involved pursuing his vision. For a man accused of being illiterate, he was clearly an intelligent and open-minded man. In addition to being self-taught, he had acquired a wealth of experience on the high seas, sailing in the Mediterranean, up to England, Ireland, and Iceland. Both self-study and practical experience allowed him to acquire a practical background in contemporary navigation tools and techniques, such as the astrolabe, compass, charting, and declination tables. Of interesting note is that his expertise in calculating lunar eclipses would later prove of great value on one of his subsequent voyages. He was also adroit in applying dead reckoning while at sea, which is hard enough on land. Dead reckoning, of course, entails using the stars, the wind, and currents to determine progress at sea.

Unlike some contemporary explorers of the time, Columbus was a moderate in all activities considered pleasurable. He drank and ate in moderation and, for the most part, was healthy, in terms of his vision and hearing. Unfortunately, the combination of age and experience in the high seas resulted in him suffering from gout, arthritis, and malaria.

What about Columbus as a visionary? How did he use his background, knowl-edge, and experience to convince patrons to buy into his vision of finding access to the east by sailing west across the Atlantic?

Christopher Columbus without a doubt was what some people would refer to as an entrepreneur. He was seeking financial backing, or venture capital, to help turn his vision into reality: finding a route to China—that is, Cathay—by sailing west across the Atlantic. He needed one or more patrons, like the artists of his day, who had the resources to help him. These patrons served as the financiers; without their help, his vision was nothing more than a dream. Just the title he called his vision reflected his entrepreneurial spirit: the "Enterprise of the Indies."

The Admiral of the Ocean, the title granted by King Ferdinand and Queen Isabella of Castile, was not a delusional man whom some members of the court and ecclesiastics accused him of being. Like many visionaries of contemporary times, he was also rebuked and rebuffed as being incorrect and impractical. However, these rejections did not stop him. As a visionary, he persisted, even being rejected by King John II of Portugal, Henry the VII of England, and Charles VIII of France before getting a second round with King Ferdinand and Queen Isabella of Spain. Sometimes a man with a burning belief in a vision is impossible to stop.

Columbus backed his vision with facts and beliefs known at the time. Like most of the educated people of the time, he did not believe the world was flat but shaped like a pear; the planet is not round but somewhat shaped like an egg. While his calculations about the distance to go from the Canary Islands to the Cathay were miscalculated, the reality was no one else knew the real distance anyway. No one knew about the large landmass that cut down the Western Hemisphere called North, Central, and South America. It is somewhat ironic that the king of Portugal ordered a group to test some of Columbus's theories in the Atlantic but failed to prove validity due to their inability to sail in inclement weather; they concluded the voyage was impossible, which may have been the result of their own poor seamanship.

Columbus did not develop his vision in a vacuum. He had access to many resources. He had nautical charts from seafaring nations, like Genoa and Portugal, and a terrestrial globe by Martin Behaim of Germany which not only showed a route from Europe to India via the Cape of Good Hope but also lands identified by Marco Polo and the legendary islands of St. Brendan and Antillia. Columbus, being religious man of the times, also had access to the works of the papacy, such as a work by Pope Pius II on circumnavigating the Africa coast and that of a cardinal of Pierre d'Ally who deduced the possibility that India and China could be reached by sailing west. Coupled with all this background information, largely conjectural, Columbus used his experience to add credence to his vision. He possessed a solid knowledge of the trade winds; spent time in the Madeiras, having married Felipa Moniz Perestrelo, daughter of a widowed wife of a captain and member of the Portuguese court, who surely had to have access to nautical charts and instruments; had sailed, for example, in the Mediterranean and probably the Celtic Sea; and likely heard about the Vikings going to Greenland. In other words, his vision was grounded in reality, supported by what was known or rumored to be true at the time.

Situation

His vision, despite being based upon the knowledge of the times, was not enough to obtain the backing he needed. He had two other factors that pushed King Ferdinand and Queen Isabella to support him. The first one was the rise of Islam, which was cutting off overland trade from the east. The other one was an upstart country called Portugal, which had a few successful voyages by going around the Cape of Good Hope, one being that of Bartolomeu Dias. Between the commercial choking by the Muslims and the competition by the Portuguese, the buy-in from Spanish patrons, or sponsors, was set. Not surprisingly, Columbus was heading to France to seek the patronage of Charles VIII when he was recalled to Spain by King Ferdinand and Queen Isabella.

Armed with his knowledge and experience and the backing of his vision, Columbus was well prepared to go on four voyages. What follows is a short overview of each voyage.

First Expedition

The first voyage, arguably the most famous of the four, started in August 1492. Christopher Columbus, having the approval of King Ferdinand and Queen Isabela, eased his way down the Rio Tinto from Palos, with *La Pinta*, *La Niña*, and *Santa María*, the third one being his flagship, to seek a route to the Indies. These vessels were quite small, being packed with a difficult group of Spaniards to manage, with the addition of three Italians, including Columbus himself. *La Niña* and *La Pinta* were captained by the Pinzon family, who would challenge his authority over the fleet. After an intermediate stop in the Canaries, specifically the island of La Gomora, for supplies, pleasure, and repairs at Las Palmas, Columbus, designated the captain-general, now followed the easterly trade winds toward what would become known as the New World. For the most part, the journey was relatively smooth as the three vessels went in pursuit of "God, Gold, and Glory."

About a month after leaving the Canary Islands, the weather turned inclement occasionally and eventually into doldrums, the search for signs of land proved fruitless, and with the threat of being trapped in a bed of seaweed in the Sargasso Sea, the crew became nervous and impatient with the progress and threatened mutiny. Columbus was able to persuade the men to give him additional time, with the promise of a reward for whoever sighted land first. Wisely, some would call duplicitous, Columbus maintained two logbooks. One that he made available for the crew to see, which underestimated the distance, and the other for himself, which showed more realistic progress. The former assuaged their concerns.

Before landing at what was named San Salvador (now Watling Island in the Bahamas) and what the Indians (the name he gave to the natives thinking he was in India) called Guanahani, the tension must have been immense among the crew considering he offered a silk doublet along with the reward of 10,000 maravedis offered by the sovereigns to the first man to spot land. Not surprisingly, the gold-hungry Spanish and Italian eyes were glued to the sea and horizon looking for signals that land was nearby, such as floating wood and birds. Even Columbus's eyes were also glued to the sea and the horizon, thinking he had spotted a light, supposedly verified by another crew member, on a distant shore. Not just any seaman could claim sighting land; the spotting required approval of one of the sovereign's supervisors on board, named Rodrigo Sanchez. On October 12, in the early morning, Columbus entered the history books, coming ashore on the island, which he named San Salvador and greeting Arawak natives, who helped him to do some additional exploring, to include Cuba (which he thought was part of China) and Hispaniola, now Haiti. On December 24, the *Santa María* hit a coral reef in Hispaniola. The captain-general decided to build a fort, named La Navidad, using the remains of the *Santa María*, on the island. Then, Columbus headed back to Spain in the midst of very inclement weather; onboard the ship were natives, sample vegetation, parrots, and a small booty of pearls and gold, along with some sailors allegedly infected with syphilis. On the return voyage, the crew of the *Niña* and *Pinta* did not have a very pleasant welcome in the Azores, in the hope of visiting a local chapel. A Portuguese officer arrested the crew for poaching, but they were released after Columbus crushed the town where they were held. Columbus then proceeded to Portugal, achieving landfall south of Lisbon, briefly showcased his achievements with the king, and then returned to Palos. A letter was sent to the sovereigns by the person responsible for procuring the funds for the 1492 expedition, Luis de Santángel, announcing the return of Columbus. Eventually, the captain-general, now Admiral of the Ocean, showcased the results of the expedition in Barcelona.

Second Expedition

The second expedition, departing in September 1493, was proof that Christopher was now at the top of the ladder of success. King Ferdinand and Queen Isabella were apparently so impressed that Columbus left on this expedition with 17 ships and approximately 1,500 men along with colonialists, with some being criminals, women available for matrimony, and a few priests to convert the natives. The cargo was not trivial in variety and size either, which included livestock and seeds. The ultimate goal was to establish trading centers; however, the expedition resembled one of conquest as much as it did commerce.

The Admiral, after a brief stop at the Canary Islands, headed toward what was known as the Lesser Antilles, which are a smaller group of islands south of the Greater Antilles, such as Cuba and Puerto Rico, based upon the guidance of the natives that he had brought aboard from the first voyage. The Lesser Antilles included St. Croix, Virgin Islands, and Dominica. The Spaniards spent a few days at an island Columbus named after his flagship, *Marigalante*, when he discovered the Caribs, then proceeded onward to Puerto Rico and arrived finally at Hispaniola.

Before returning to Hispaniola, he returned to La Navidad, where Columbus encountered a gruesome sight. The original crew members who stayed were dead, killed by the natives under the name of a Taino cacique named Caonabo over the Spaniards' treatment of native women and being consumed with gold fever. Taking a hint, Columbus decided to find a safer place to set up the trading center.

The experience on Hispaniola was not the most pleasant, either, with about 20 percent of the Spaniards falling ill. An expedition into the interior discovered enough gold along with spices that he decided to return 12 of the 17 vessels in his fleet along with about two dozen natives to Spain. He also set up a small port with his brother Diego in charge of a council while Columbus went exploring, convinced that he was getting closer to discovering the route to China. Meanwhile, Diego and his brother Bartholomew had to deal with the repeated problem of the Spaniards being infected with gold fever and not treating the natives very well. Columbus decided to return to Spain with more natives, beyond the 500 or so ones he had sent back earlier, only this time with the purpose of selling them as slaves. The samples of gold and other artifacts brought back by Columbus were enough to spur the sovereign's interest in continuing the expeditions.

Third Expedition

This expedition took a little more time to get underway. What was the rush, with Diego and Bartholomew in charge, right? Apparently, unbeknownst to the Admiral, the situation in Hispaniola was deteriorating and so was his competency as an administrator. In May 1948, Columbus began this expedition with a smaller number of vessels, thinking once again that he was getting closer to realizing his vision of reaching Asia. Departing with a smaller fleet than that of the second expedition, Columbus returned to Hispaniola, departing from Sanlúcar de Barrameda, stopping at the Canary Islands and Cape Verde and then off to Hispaniola. However, he discovered Trinidad and went ashore on the Paria Peninsula of Venezuela, still thinking that he was close to the Indies, viewing it as part of Indonesia. When he arrived at Santo Domingo, he discovered something he probably did not want to see: the settlement there was in turmoil. The Spaniards once again were taken over with gold fever and mistreating the natives. What was even worse was that he discovered that his brothers, Diego and Bartholomew, had lost control, facing a rebellion by the Spaniards themselves. What was even still worse was that the sovereigns received word about the turmoil and sent Francisco de Bobadilla to restore order, which he did. However, Bobadilla made compromises with his fellow Spaniards (something Columbus tried to do but failed) but was not so kind with Columbus and his two brothers. He placed all three men in chains. While onboard the ship and upon return in 1500 to Cadiz, Columbus continued to wear the chains as if carrying a cross. Eventually, he removed the chains upon orders of King Ferdinand and Queen Isabela who sent a governor to the Indies with a large fleet and a substantial quantity of colonists. Columbus still clung to the belief that he could find the route to China if given one more opportunity, which he did receive.

Fourth Expedition

This expedition, beginning in 1500, was as exciting as the previous ones but proved disastrous. Columbus, still a supreme navigator and an incompetent administrator, was no longer a viceroy, was now returning to the Caribbean, convinced he was close to finding the route to Asia via the Gulf of Mexico. The expedition was a dangerous one because he was forbidden to return to Hispaniola. Columbus, believing a hurricane was impending, tried to enter Santo Domingo to warn the governor but to no avail. Columbus was not allowed back to Hispaniola, and the governor nevertheless decided to send a fleet of 29 ships loaded with gold back to Spain. The hurricane devastated the fleet, losing most of the vessels, crew, and gold. As for Columbus, he had found protection near Santo Domingo and then proceeded on his journey along the coast of Central America in search of his vision. He sailed along the coasts of countries known today as Nicaragua, Costa Rica, and Panama. As fate would have it, he came close to finding that route near the spot where the north entrance of the Panama Canal exists today, at Limon Bay. Columbus continued to cruise down channels, only to find he had to turn back. The insects, and rain too, had become intolerable. While traveling along the coast of Panama, he established a trading post that he called Santa María de Belén where he mined for gold and repaired his vessels. He interacted with the natives, who presented large gold artifacts and jewelry. Once again, the Spaniard's lust for gold and other pleasures consumed them, and the relationship with the natives went haywire. The natives attacked under the leadership of cacique Quibían, giving Columbus no other choice but to depart.

Then came more problems. The *Vizcaina* was abandoned due to worms destroying the hull of the vessel. Columbus then sailed toward Jamaica where he and his crew were marooned in what is known as the Bay of Santa Gloria. Columbus, the great navigator and seaman, found himself and his crew marooned; the only saving grace was Hispaniola, where he was prohibited from going ashore. Twice he attempted to send a messenger to Hispaniola. The first attempt failed, but the second one succeeded. In addition, many of the Spaniards were again becoming difficult to control; some seized canoes and tried to make for Hispaniola but failed in the attempt.

For a while, the relationship with the natives was fine. Then food became scarce, and the natives were no longer interested in trading food for trinkets, like bells.

The relationship with the natives was becoming increasingly tenuous. Columbus, who knew a lunar eclipse was impending, used the event to his advantage to scare the natives into providing food by communicating to God of his displeasure. The trick worked, but Columbus had other problems.

The second messenger would return but not for several months. Columbus and his crew waited for more than a half a year. The governor of Hispaniola decided to send a caravel to not only rescue the members of the crew but also Columbus and his son Diego. Columbus chartered a vessel to take them back to Sanlúcar in 1504, not realizing that he had almost found the future access route, albeit man-made, to Asia: the Panama Canal.

Lessons

So, what are some of the key lessons that project managers can learn (Figure 2.1) from the experience of Christopher Columbus?

Be persistent when pursuing a vision. Columbus persevered despite the rejection he received from quite a few sovereigns, such as King John II of Portugal and Charles VIII of France. Also, during the pursuit of that vision, the people, mainly the Spaniards, who did help him to make the Enterprise of the Indies a reality, did not seem to share in it, at least not in total; gold appeared to be their only motivator or, at minimum, putting God and glory a distant second. Still, Columbus persevered even when his realization of the vision seemed impossible to achieve. Even on his deathbed, Columbus believed that he discovered a portion of the Indies.

Base a vision on the knowledge and technology of the times. The Admiral's vision was based upon the knowledge and technology of his time. The vision was based upon papal works, experiences of other seaman, his own experience, legends, and mapmakers. He faced two challenges at the time. The real challenge was the limited knowledge that existed and the primitive technology (compared to today's) that he used to turn his vision into reality. He combined speculation and facts to garner the necessary sponsorship to take the first voyage.

The Lessons of Christopher Columbus

- Be persistent when pursuing a vision
- Base a vision on the knowledge and technology of the times
- Challenge the prevailing paradigm
- Combine vision with action
- Obtain buy-in from key stakeholders, including subordinates
- Avoid the danger of inflexibility; do not ignore reality
- Do not rely on family at the exclusion of more competent others

Figure 2.1 The Lessons of Christopher Columbus.

Challenge the prevailing paradigm. Despite his religiosity, which took hold of just about everyone at the time, Columbus maintained an inquisitive mind. His expeditions occurred during the time of the Renaissance when scientific and rediscovery of Grecian thinking challenged the status quo. Columbus did not subscribe to superstitions and questioned contemporary religious paradigms that were held by powerful leaders. He persisted, formulating a vision that eventually changed the world.

Combine vision with action. Columbus is often portrayed as someone with a nebulous vision that was locked up in his head. The reality was that he took the vision and determined what was required to achieve it. He did his research and recorded the results in his logbooks. He used his practical experience and his knowledge to develop the vision. He was an expert navigator and seaman, one of the best at the time, and he used knowledge and experience to try to turn his vision into a reality, attempting four times and coming close on the fourth trip. In a sense, he did achieve part of the vision but was stymied by court politics and unruly crews.

Obtain buy-in of a vision from key stakeholders, including subordinates. Columbus did receive buy-in of his vision from senior sponsors after a long period of rejection. He gained the title of Admiral of the Ocean and a significant share of the metals from lands he discovered. The problem was that the crew, a significant stakeholder, did not buy into the vision. The Spaniards clearly bought into part of the vision, which was gold, but that was about it. In time, as reflected with Bobadilla coming to Hispaniola to bring order, the crew only shared in part of the vision. The insurrection soon permeated the sovereign's court.

Avoid the danger of inflexibility of a vision; in other words, do not ignore reality. While his perseverance was impressive by any standard, Columbus often became obsessed with the vision almost to the point of being ludicrous. Even on his deathbed, he did not concede that his vision needed modification. Even when Pinzon recommended modifying the course on the first voyage, Columbus refused to yield, with his vision taking him to San Salvador rather than what would have been Florida. Throughout all four voyages, Columbus believed that he had reached the outskirts of Asia. Having a vision is useful to plan and execute an expedition but being inflexible can cause problems, especially if unrealistic. If the vision remains unchanged, the plan will likely become unrealistic, as it did for Columbus.

Do not rely on family at the exclusion of others when pursuing a vision. Columbus by all accounts was an inadequate administrator and lacked political sophistication. When he put his brothers, Diego and Bartholomew, in charge of Hispaniola while he pursued gold and a route to China, the Spaniards revolted. They had no buy-in in the running of the island, which resulted in the mistreatment of the natives. In other words, even a great visionary needs the support of sponsors and the people doing the work.

Final Thoughts

Christopher Columbus remains a lightning rod of controversy from the time of his expedition to the present day. He was a man with a burning vision when few at the time had one or were stuck in a stifling paradigm about how the world worked. He was not mad, though some to this day may think so. He was not ignorant, while others still think so. He had a vision that many understood but few wanted to embrace. Still, he persisted, and the Western Hemisphere for better or worse reflects that vision.

To a large extent, many project managers suffer the same fate. The only difference is the vision is given to them to turn into reality. Few people, sometimes even the person who came up with the vision, have more than a vague idea of what it is. Like Don Quixote, the vision appears to many stakeholders as nothing more than a windmill. But not to the originator of the vision, for whom it is all too real. The project manager then must turn that vision into a reality, and if he or she fails to turn it into a reality, the person will face the same fate as Columbus, a man with a vision that few accepted at the time.

Chapter 3

Henry the Navigator: Being a Sponsor

Providing the necessary support, financial and other means, to ensure achievement of a vision.

A strange fact of history: few people outside of Europe have any idea who Prince Henry, the third son of King João I, was or what historical significance he had. Yet, he was instrumental in furthering European exploration by sponsoring expeditions in the Atlantic and the west coast of Africa. If anyone needed a great sponsor, Prince Henry was the man.

Background

What kind of man was Henry who played such a significant role not only in the history of Portugal but also of the Western world? He was a man of many contradictions who was born in 1394 and died in 1460. He would lavishly spend his country's wealth to achieve his goals and put on expensive festive events. Yet, he lived modestly, living ascetically, and was known to have kept his virginity to the very end. He was a religious zealot, reflected in his religious incursions and expeditions. He was, according to many, a very devout man who was impulsive and obstinate, which led, contradictorily, to the raping and pillaging of a Muslim city in Morocco. Nevertheless, he was a visionary who was realistic, becoming a masterful strategist and tactical planner along with being a skillful organizer. He was tolerant of other peoples, even willing to have them join his incursions and expeditions yet had no qualms about maximizing wealth not just through spices and gold but also slavery.

DOI: 10.1201/9781003028734-3

Most interestingly, he had such a keen interest in expeditions but never went on one himself. One aspect of his personality that proved useful in pursuing his vision of religious conquest against the Muslims and amassing wealth to pursue his expeditions was increasing his power. Another aspect is that he had a strong sense of destiny not just for himself but also for Portugal. He achieved that by sponsoring incursions and expeditions, the result of his boldness and imaginative visions.

Prince Henry was also the son of Philippa of Lancaster whose marriage to King João I forged an alliance with the English. The relationship between King João I and Philippa would prove to be of great help to Henry when sponsoring not just expeditions but also attacking the Muslims in Morocco, especially against the attack of the Moroccan city of Ceuta in 1415. King João I's foray against the Moroccans would have a lasting impact on Henry as a future sponsor. Henry played a significant role in the attack, albeit experiencing a host of problems as a leader, to include dealing with disease and seasickness among the troops, the vagaries of the wind and weather, and navigational problems. Despite these and many other obstacles, Henry by all accounts exhibited good and bad qualities. Bravery, a key characteristic of any warrior, he did not lack; however, he also showed some weaknesses, such as being impatient and impulsive, as well as failing to exhibit good strategic and tactical knowledge. However, to some extent, he managed to control these weaknesses, even to overcome them, in the future. What was even more important though, is what he saw during the assault. Ceuta was a rich city, being a major trading center in the Sahara. Spices, oil, tapestries, and slaves were just a few of the riches in the city. More importantly, it had a great quantity of gold. He noticed that the riches were an excellent way to motivate the troops, which encouraged them to ransack the city.

He also recognized another motivator, religion, which also justified the attack. Not surprisingly, he proceeded to turn the major mosque in Ceuta into a Christian church. King João I had also laid the groundwork for Henry from a religious perspective. The king and Philippa ensured that a papal bull gave an additional religious justification. Philippa was also deeply religious, giving Prince Henry a fragment of a cross to carry into battle, which occurred just prior to her death.

Hence, gold and religion became useful motivators. Henry learned some key lessons that would serve him well in the future. One of the most important lessons was not being particularly prejudiced against using people from other cultures at that time. His troops consisted of people from England, Italian city-states (such as Genoa), Castilians, Germans, and the Flemish. His willingness to work with anyone to achieve whatever he had in mind would serve him well in the future.

As a result of his superb performance against Ceuta, King João I made him the Duke of Viseu. This honor gave him a strong appreciation for the importance of position and power in sponsoring his expeditions. Eventually, he acquired other notable titles that granted him more power, authority, and wealth, which, in turn, helped him in sponsoring expeditions.

Prince Henry was now on the road to achieving even more greatness, at least according to his astrologers. He did not travel down the road of destiny haphazardly. At Sagres in Portugal, he established what would be known as a research and development center. It became a mariner's delight, serving as a place to accumulate and share knowledge and experience about cartography, shipbuilding, and navigation. He invited people from all walks of life who served his needs for expeditions. Some were sailors and shipbuilders while others were simply travelers. Even people from other nationalities and ethnicities were not exempted, for example, Jews and Muslims, Italians, and Africans. One of his brothers, Pedro, even went on an excursion throughout Europe collecting information about Marco Polo and his travels, as well as acquiring Italian maps. He had all his explorers keep copious notes and maps in logbooks and charts. He even obtained and developed navigation techniques and instruments, such as the quadrant, to address complications in determining latitude. But one key invention was the long triangular lateen sail, which enabled greater speed and mobility of his caravels; the lateen sail was really based upon the vessels that sailed in the eastern part of the Mediterranean. Soon Lagos in Portugal became a major shipbuilding center. Henry became an innovator, using the knowledge and expertise of others to embark on expeditions.

The prince was a realist. He knew that he needed to increase his wealth, not just acquire more knowledge. Sacking Ceuta was just not enough, especially for someone who tended to spend more than what was at his disposal. Prince Henry needed to acquire more financial and nonfinancial resources. In addition to Sagres, he leveraged his knowledge, existing resources, and victories to embark on expeditions.

Situation

Prince Henry's contributions are better appreciated by understanding the status of Portugal at the time. Portugal was a fledgling country, formed after a conflict with Spain; the small country was formed in 1385 but really did not truly become independent until 1411. The consequences of this independence were immense. Portugal was a poor country riddled with inflation. It also had little or no access to the Mediterranean, while other countries had trading relationships with the Muslims, despite the Ottoman Turks having a virtual monopolistic stranglehold on all maritime and overland routes with the Italians, such as the Genoese, being the conveyors of two important items: spices and gold. With Spain to the immediate east, Italians in the Mediterranean, and Muslims in the near east and north Africa, Portugal almost had no other choice but to sail west in the Atlantic and down the west African coast. Lacking wealth and access to routes, the Portuguese had to pursue a different route to riches. Fortunately, Portugal was united at least in comparison with other areas of Europe being wracked with religious wars and power struggles. The first step for Portugal was to break the stranglehold of those infidels—that is, the Muslims. The men to do just that were King João I and his sons, especially Prince Henry, who was officially known as Infante Dom Henrique, o Navegador.

Expeditions

Some of the first targets of his expeditions were islands in the Atlantic Ocean, specifically the Azores, Madeiras, and Canaries. He viewed the islands as more of a source of wealth to enable expeditions along the west coast of Africa. For example, Madeira, meaning wood in Portuguese, provided a resource for building caravels. Wood was, however, only one source of wealth for Prince Henry. The Madeiras provided materials for dye. The Azores provided resources to pay for his expeditions. While the Madeiras and the Azores were colonized without, for the most part, colonial claims by Spain, the Canaries had enough undiscovered islands that it caused conflict between the two countries. Portugal colonized the Canaries, which ended up as bases to continue expeditions along the west coast of Africa. For example, the Portuguese explorer Alvise Cadamosto (who happened to be Venetian with the name of Luigi da Mosta) stopped at the Madeira and Canary Islands on one of the trips down the west coast of Africa. Cadamosto even discovered some islands by accident, the Cape Verde Islands and, subsequently, Senegaland. Cadamosta was just one of the examples of Prince Henry displaying a willingness to have the services of competent people from other ethnicities and nationalities to execute his expeditions. At times, too, he would include the services of his squires if he felt he could trust their competency, such as the services of Dinís Dias, whom he sent to Senegal to obtain slaves.

Despite his religious zealotry and his belief in astrology, Prince Henry did not hesitate to shatter fears and prejudices when it came to expeditions. At Sagres, he took on the common fear that the magnetic compass was not some "possessed" device to fear. The biggest fear that he had to overcome was the one that permeated mariners: the impossibility of passing Cape Bojador off the west coast of Africa without being turned black or burned up by the intense temperatures. Gil Eannes failed in his first attempt and returned. Prince Henry believed it was not impossible and gave Eannes an incentive to try a second time, in 1434, where he sailed into the Atlantic Ocean and then back toward Africa and passed Cape Bojador, proving Prince Henry was right.

Once the fears of Cape Bojador were circumvented, Prince Henry continued expeditions down the west coast of Africa. The expeditions became bolder and more frequent, often lucrative but not always. Increasingly, slavery became as lucrative as gold. In fact, the latter became so lucrative that expeditions, now under King Pedro, granted Prince Henry exclusive rights south of Bojador and entitled him to have one-fifth of any cargo. The prince was now emboldened, sending explorers in search of the Rio de Ouro, the Senegal River, where what was known as a silent trade occurred that involved traders like the Moroccans, now the Portuguese, piling trinkets perceived as valuable by natives, who left gold in exchange but only after vacating the site. The 1440s and 1450s became an intense period for Portuguese exploration as the scope expanded farther down the west coast of Africa.

Prince Henry, of course, knew that he needed more than gold and slaves to justify his expeditions. He needed reasons that would further justify his expeditions. After all, what would happen if the sources of gold and slaves evaporated? The justification was religious. Conversion of natives would not, however, be enough. He also needed the support of powerful religious powers in Europe as King João did to justify the invasion of Ceuta. He was now the leader of the Order of Christ in Portugal, which gave him additional access to wealth to finance his expeditions. But he also had the support of the pope, who issued a papal bull granting Prince Henry and the king power to address spiritual matters south of Cape Bojador.

Prince Henry was not perfect as a sponsor. Sometimes, his arrogance consumed him. He sent unsuccessful expeditions up rivers, like the Senegal and Niger, with the purpose of joining the fictitious Prester John along the Nile to defeat the Muslims in Jerusalem. His religious zealotry resulted in a terrible defeat while attempting to conquer Tangier.

All toll, however, Henry was a good sponsor. His efforts laid the groundwork for more successful expeditions long after his death, to include Bartolomeu Dias sailing around the Cape of Good Hope and Vasco da Gama making it to India. In the end, Prince Henry turned Portugal into a colonial-going concern, leading to an empire that included, in part or whole, Brazil, Angola, Mozambique, India, and China.

Lessons

So, what are some of the key lessons (Figure 3.1) about sponsors that project managers learn from the experiences of Prince Henry?

The Lessons of Henry the Navigator

- Stick to the vision but avoid inflexibility
- Leverage the knowledge and expertise of others
- Provide the necessary financial and intangible support
- Be persistent in the face of opposition and fear
- Build alliances
- Provide a good incentive plan
- Capitalize on failure as much as success
- Avoid ethnocentricity

Figure 3.1   The Lessons of Henry the Navigator.

Stick to the vision but avoid inflexibility. The prince knew what he wanted and attempted to merge two goals: spreading Christianity and gaining from expeditions. Sometimes the two goals supported one another, such as pursuing gold and converting natives to Christianity. Other times, he used religious zealotry to pursue goals like looking for Pester John in Ethiopia and marching on to Jerusalem. These expeditions wasted resources that could have been better allocated to more meaningful expeditions. In other words, sometimes he was dissipating his energies and finding himself scrambling for resources.

Leverage the knowledge and expertise of others. Prince Henry was a professional par excellence in this regard. He had people from all backgrounds come to Sagres to contribute their knowledge, wisdom, and experience in a way that would enhance his vision and expeditions, whether it included developing maps or inventing or improving navigational experiences. By doing so, he took advantage of technological advancements.

Provide the necessary financial and intangible support. He used his wealth, position, and relationships to support his expeditions. He knew wealth was only one means of support. He was, however, shrewd enough to know that people also needed ways to justify their actions and keep them motivated during times of stress. In his case, he found religion as the vehicle to do just that, especially during expeditions resulting in disappointments, such as sailing caravels down African rivers to pursue the fictitious Prester John.

Be persistent in the face of opposition and fear. Not everyone embraced the prince's incursions and expeditions. His incursion against Tangier ended in failure in part because of a lack of support. Overcoming fear was even harder, as demonstrated when he pushed for explorers to pass Cape Bojador or even having mariners be willing to work with a magnetic compass. He was what would be considered today as a change agent.

Build alliances. Prince Henry knew he needed allies, or stakeholders, to help him succeed; he needed others to buy into to his vision which, in turn, enabled him to be an excellent sponsor. Two of these stakeholders were King João I and the papacy. He also had the support of organizations that he also controlled, such as the Order of Christ.

Provide a good incentive plan. When Eannes returned after failing to pass Cape Bojador, Prince Henry offered additional incentives, which were apparently lucrative enough that the explorer was willing to venture farther out into the turbulent Atlantic Ocean to get that reward. He also compensated other explorers, which, in turn, enhanced Henry's wealth by collecting the royal fifth. If wealth was not enough, a papal bull added an additional incentive.

Capitalize on failure as much as success. Prince Henry, like all good sponsors, had some expeditions that, quite frankly, were failures. Already were mentioned the ones like linking up with Prester John, who never existed. On some expeditions that failed, Prince Henry was still able to acquire useful knowledge from the experiences. He expected all his explorers to record details in logbooks, update navigation charts, and record observations about potential lucrative opportunities that might exist. All this knowledge was used to plan additional explorations.

Avoid ethnocentricity. One of the most impressive aspects of Prince Henry was his willingness to engage people with expertise who came from all over. He used Italians, such as Venetians, to lead expeditions. He obtained the services of a Catalan Jew from Majorca, Spain, to assemble a plethora of geographic information from returning explorers. He obtained insights from Muslims and Africans arriving in Sagres and Lagos. What mattered to Prince Henry were the vision and goals that motivated him to sponsor expeditions, and he was willing to provide the necessary support.

Final Thoughts

Henry the Navigator knew what was necessary to turn his expeditions into a success. He knew what was necessary. He developed and applied technology on the expeditions that he supported. He was willing to do whatever it took, financial or in-kind, to ensure that his expeditions succeeded. With each expedition, he took chances building on the experiences of each expedition and taking them one step farther, discovering and revealing the west coast of Africa from a European perspective.

Many project managers would love a sponsor like Henry the Navigator. Quite a few project managers never receive the same level of support from their sponsors. Few sponsors are willing to invest the time, money, and effort to ensure their projects succeed. Often, sponsors want results faster, better, and cheaper despite all the analysis presented by their project managers that realistically this cannot happen when the schedule is compressed and given a shoestring budget. Many project managers would gain a great deal by having sponsors like Henry the Navigator.

Chapter 4

Ferdinand Magellan: Focusing on the Goal

Defining a goal and concentrating on achieving it.

Imagine leading a fleet of five ships to go to the other side of the world. Some crew members, including a few captains of those vessels, are on the verge of mutiny. Many crew members do not recognize your command, objecting because you are of a certain nationality. You force men to eat leather and biscuits filled with worms; the bilge water stinks. Rats crawl on and under the deck; when caught, the rats are fed to the crew. Squalls and fierce gales threaten to capsize any one of the vessels. You have only six months of food to sustain the voyage after being told you had at least two years available. At any moment, you could have your throat slit and pushed into the dark depths of the Atlantic or Pacific Ocean. At any time, one of the vessels can simply leave the fleet without you knowing it. Finally, after all of this happening, you reach your destination, and then you are killed.

Welcome to the world of Ferdinand Magellan, a Portuguese explorer who became a Spaniard and changed the world forever. Magellan was a man of supreme resolve who had one goal in mind: to sail from Spain, across the Atlantic Ocean, through a strait, now known as the Strait of Magellan, which cut through the tip of South America. He then proceeded onward to an ocean that he called Pacific because of the relative calmness of the waves, naming it so after comparing it to the Atlantic Ocean, and then he reached the Spice Islands.

DOI: 10.1201/9781003028734-4

Background

Since he was a member of the nobility, Magellan, known in Portugal as Fernão de Magalhães, had access to the court of Portugal, that of Queen Leonora. This experience prepared him for future endeavors. In addition to being a page, he also attended what people today would refer to as "fork and knife school." He learned some important skills of a warrior in those times, such as hunting, riding a horse, using swords, and seamanship.

Competent and only 25 years old, now on his way to becoming a seasoned warrior and seaman, he was ready to serve the king, and off he went serving in the fleet of Dom Francisco de Almeida, an explorer and viceroy of India. On the way, Almeida set up many trading bases on the east coast of Africa and the west coast of India, capturing and destroying cities. Magellan increased his military expertise, participating in a naval war between Portugal and the Egyptians and Venetians. While boarding a ship, he was severely injured, but that did not stop him.

He continued to serve the king of Portugal by engaging in warfare in Malacca in 1509 and was promoted to captain due to his performance. In 1510, he exhibited more leadership in a different way. His vessel hit a shoal in the Maldives during the night but managed to reach a small island using parts of the wreckage of the vessel; the other officers built a vessel out of the wreckage and then left. But not Magellan; he did not desert the others on the island, remaining until everyone was rescued. If that experience was not enough, in 1511, Magellan commanded a fleet of three ships to help conquer Malacca and managed to seize a large booty. During this time, he also seized a young teenage slave whom he named Henrique de Malaca, who tagged along until Magellan's death. Magellan subsequently exceeded his orders by sailing farther east and, consequently, was relieved of command and returned to Lisbon as a lowly usher after previously being promoted to captain and elevated in nobility to the level of fidalgo escudeiro (noble squire).

His luck was slowly starting to change, only not for the better. Magellan felt a need to command at sea once again. Instead of returning to the Malaccas, he received the opportunity to fight against the Moors in northern Africa and received a wound in the leg, causing him to limp for life. His career opportunities, at least in Portugal, were over. However, they were not in Spain. Magellan decided to pursue opportunities in Spain.

Situation

Portugal and Spain were vying for territory under the guides of gold, God, and glory. To add to the rivalry, the declaration of Pope Alexander VI, under the Treaty of Tordesillas, split the world into two halves in terms of exploration: Spain was allowed all lands to the west and Portugal to the east. Obviously, the knowledge of what lay beyond was limited because the two would sooner or later encounter one another in a world that is round, not flat.

The trade in spices was not an easy matter during that time, and the handling fees to acquire spices, including other precious items, such as gold and jewels, were for the time quite exorbitant. Small boats, ships, camels, and men all were involved in the Malay Peninsula. Indians, Arabs, and Venetians not only added to the price of the goods eventually making it to Europe but also the unpredictability of delivery due to danger from man and nature.

Magellan, therefore, decided not to make a career change; rather, he would make a nationality change; he became Spanish along with a name change to Hernando de Magallanes. Magellan did not take the leap alone. He brought along his slave and a prominent cosmographer and mathematician, Ruy de Faleira.

Magellan, a man of nobility and an experienced seaman, was a name to take seriously. His status helped him paved the way to propose a voyage to Charles V of Spain. Magellan became friends with an important person named Duarte Barbosa, a Portuguese pilot working for the Spanish king. Just as importantly, Magellan became acquainted with Diogo, Barbosa's uncle, who helped pave the way to King Charles, as well as marrying Beating Barbosa in 1517. Magellan then approached the Casa de Contratación, an agency of the crown, to which he explained his plans to discover the shortest route to the Spice Islands. The plans were relayed to Magellan then on to the king's ministers and eventually coming to the attention of King Charles V.

In the background occurring in Magellan's favor, too, was some jockeying in the Spanish court. Juan Rodriguez de Fonseca, the bishop of Burgos and the controller of the Casa de Contratación, was the person who approved expeditions for the crown. He saw the value of the Spice Islands but could not get the court to embrace his plans; however, he saw Magellan as his path to convince the court of the value of the islands.

The king was receptive more toward Magellan than Faliero because of the latter's temperamental personality. Apparently, King Charles V preferred Magellan's slave over Faleiro, who happened to bring along his Sumatran wife, who also received the king's approval.

Expedition

A few preliminaries needed resolution before preparations for the expedition could commence. The terms and conditions agreed upon included Charles V paying for the expedition, which included 20,000 ducats, goods for bartering, and provisions. Magellan and Faleiro would receive 5 percent of the profits, and their heirs would govern any discovered lands and have the title of adelantados (civil-military governors). Faleiro was never able to benefit from the contract, being sacked by Charles V, but did eventually receive some compensation.

Magellan received five vessels under his command. These were the *Trinidad* (the flagship), *San Antonio*, *Concepción*, *Victoria*, and *Santiago*. The crew was approximately 250 men of various ethnicities and nationalities, which included Spaniards, Portuguese, Genoese, Sicilians, French, Flemings, Germans, Greeks, Negroes, Malaysians, and English. This mixed crew would eventually pose a serious challenge to Magellan's command of his ships; the challenges would come from both his captains and crew. Magellan also received provisions for what he thought was for two years, only to later discover that it would last for approximately six months. He did receive a medley of items to barter with natives, which included knives, brass bracelets, hawks' bells, and fishhooks. The vessels were also equipped with navigational tools, including charts, compasses, quadrants, astrolabes, and hourglasses, as well as a wide array of armaments.

Magellan was now ready for the expedition that was originally rejected by King Manuel of Portugal and now embraced by Charles V. He was also now a father of a son named Rodrigo who had been knighted by the king, becoming knight commander of the Military Order of Santiago. This situation only increased the jealousy of some members of Charles V's court toward Magellan.

One would think Magellan's problems were behind him. He had turned a lemon into lemonade, so to speak. He was now ready to focus on achieving his goals. He had someone lurking in the background, however, determined to stop Magellan—King Manuel of Portugal. The Portuguese king had suppliers bribed to create a shortage of provisions for the voyage, which he had succeeded in doing so. He also looked askance at a known plot to murder Magellan, even though a rumor circulated that the king was behind it. Finally, as the fleet left to discover the strait leading to the Spice Islands, the Portuguese king sent his own fleet to stop Magellan, but it was unable to reach the latter in time.

Magellan was ready to realize his vision that had these goals in mind: sail westward, discover the strait cutting through South America, and sail on to the Spice Islands. He was determined nothing was going to stop him, not even an assassin or a king.

Reaching his vision and goals was not going to be easy. He and his crew were going to face unimaginable hardships. His resolve would be his biggest asset and his greatest liability.

In September 1519, Magellan departed from Spain, sailing along the coast of West Africa using Tenerife, in the Canary Islands, as a resupply point and then passing the Cape Verde Islands. Already, problems began to surface. The seeds of mutiny began to grow while at the same time experiencing bad severe weather, which is common during the fall in the Atlantic. The dissent started with one of his captains, Juan de Cartegna, who was a relative of Juan Rodriguez de Fonseca and the commander of the San Antonio. Magellan, not allowing anything or anyone to stop him, placed the captain in iron restraints. Magellan continued toward South America and followed along its coast. He reached the location of Rio in December, interacting briefly with the natives, and then continued onward to look for the strait but to no avail. Magellan would use an approach that would work eventually by looking for the strait; he sent smaller vessels to conduct a reconnaissance of a potential river that was not the strait. In March 1520, the captain-general decided to lay low for the winter off Port San Julian, close to the tip of South America.

Magellan anticipated that to survive the winter would require rationing, which logistically makes sense. Unfortunately, this action only pushed the seeds of mutiny through the surface. This moment became the first inflection point that would determine the future fate of the voyage. The crews of three ships erupted along with their captains. Magellan took rigorous, decisive, and stern action that would earmark him as a determined man. Captains Mendoza of the *Victoria*, Gasper de Quesada of the *Concepción*, and Cartegna of the *San Antonio* joined the revolt, requesting, along with the mutinous crew members, to return to Spain. Captain Mendoza mocked Magellan and paid with his life after laughing at the captain-general. Captain Quesada surrendered after firing a cannon that hit the vessel. Captain Cartegna surrendered to Magellan. Probably because of his relationship with Juan Rodriquez de Fonseca, Cartegna was marooned, not killed, along with a priest. Magellan held a trial, a court-martial in military parlance, and temporarily put the mutinous crew members in irons while they performed their responsibilities.

More determined than ever, Magellan continued his search for the strait, identifying an inlet that he named the Tierra de Fuego after seeing natives burning fires. He sent two vessels on a reconnaissance, which was not the strait. Once again, the crew acted up, only this time, they were willing to go to the Indies via the Cape of Good Hope. Naturally, Magellan disagreed, even in the face of a serious shortage of provisions. He backtracked, heading north.

Magellan, now with only four vessels because the *Santiago* was wrecked on a sandbar and was abandoned, continued onward looking for the strait. He discovered what would later be called the Strait of Magellan. He sent two vessels, the *San Antonio* and *Concepción*, to explore the strait, which revealed two outlets. One of the vessels returned—namely, the *Concepcion*. However, the *San Antonio* was missing. Magellan, as he did many years earlier, did not abandon his men but tried to find the *San Antonio* and failed, assuming the vessel was wrecked. Unbeknownst to him the San Antonio had been taken over by a person envious of Magellan and was returning to Spain.

Nevertheless, Magellan continued to demonstrate his resolve. He had achieved his first goal while facing numerous obstacles. He held a council, as was customary, with his officers. Most of them wanted to turn back for lack of sufficient provisions. Magellan, undeterred, disagreed, knowing all too well he probably had destroyed his relationship with Juan Rodriquez de Fonseca after marooning his nephew and not completing the voyage. The next step was to get to the Spice Islands.

The expedition, now becoming a destination, would not be an easy one either for Magellan or the crews manning the remaining vessels. The travel across the body of water that he called the Pacific was slow due to the doldrums, while the crews suffered from hunger, being forced to eat rats, leather, and worm-ridden biscuits, while others faced the wrath of scurvy. Fortunately, the fleet encountered two islands that provided some relief from hunger. After a long period, the fleet made it to the Marianas. On the island of Guam, during March 1521, the fleet provisioned itself after close to a hundred days sailing the Pacific. At first, Magellan and the crews received a warm welcome. He initially named the islands the Islas las Velas. However, after the natives pilfered the vessels, he named the islands the Ladrones, which translated means thieves. After replenishing the fleet with provisions, Magellan and his vessels departed, heading toward the Philippines.

Magellan spotted, in March, the island of Samar and then eventually landed on Homonhon Island to resupply. Then, he proceeded to Limasawa Island in the Leyte Gulf where he met first with some natives. Enrique, his slave, spoke to the natives in Malaysian, and they responded in-kind, confirming to Magellan he had made it to the Spice Islands. The natives and crew had a friendly relationship, resulting in the ruler of the island, Rajah Kolambu, coming aboard Magellan's ship. Kolambu suggested that Magellan should go to the island of Cebu, which was more prosperous. Magellan then proceeded to Cebu in April and was greeted by Sultan Humabon. The two leaders supposedly took a liking to each other, so much so that the sultan was baptized. Magellan, deciding to show his appreciation, agreed to participate in a squabble between the sultan and the chief of Mactan Island, which proved disastrous for Magellan and his crew. The captain-general, with a small contingent, landed on Mactan and was defeated. Magellan was killed; however, not without a fight. The tragedy was not just the killing of Magellan, though it was such an event. The real tragedy was that many of his men deserted him, a culmination of a series of desertions and mutinies that imperiled this expedition from the very beginning. His body was abandoned. What added to the tragedy was Enrique, Magellan's slave, who cooperated with Sultan Homabon by inviting the remaining Spaniards to a dinner. About 40 members of the crew attended the event, only to have the Filipinos turn on them. The screams echoed all the way to the vessels as some crew members managed to flee for their lives. The officers selected a new captain-general, who was subsequently replaced by Gonzalo Gómez de Espinosa who returned the two remaining vessels, the *Trinidad* and *Victoria*, to the Spice Islands in November 1521. Ironically, the *Victoria*, under the command of Juan Sebastián de Elcano, was the vessel that made it back to Seville in September 1522, while the *Trinidad*, the flagship of Magellan, remained behind, which seemed like a final betrayal of Ferdinand Magellan.

Lessons

So, what are some of the key lessons (Figure 4.1) project managers can learn from Ferdinand Magellan's experience when focusing on a goal?

Keep the goal in the forefront of your mind. Magellan knew the importance of focusing. When others, including his direct reports, wanted to return even after

The Lessons of Ferdinand Magellan

- Keep the goal in the forefront of your mind
- Expect resistance the longer the goal takes to achieve
- Be aware an estimate does not imply accuracy
- Be flexible in the pursuit of the goal
- Prepare to make unpopular decisions
- Be aware of one's own personality faults that can degrade situational awareness when pursuing a goal
- Recognize leading multinational groups can become quite challenging

Figure 4.1   The Lessons of Ferdinand Magellan.

discovering the strait for which he was named, the desire to turn back infected just about everyone but him. His vision, coupled with his goals, sustained him to the end of his life.

Expect resistance the longer the goal takes to achieve. Sometimes achieving a goal does not happen immediately. Many crew members failed to have the patience to continue. The mutinies occurred even during the trip across the Atlantic Ocean. The crews' realization that provisions were limited only made many of them want to quit as they traversed down the coast of South America. It was not until Magellan demonstrated the necessary resolve to suppress insubordination by whatever means necessary that he was able to reach his two goals, finding the strait and arriving at the Spice Islands. Interestingly, the trip across the Atlantic Ocean was shorter than the one across the Pacific Ocean but most of the insubordination and mutinies occurred when crossing the former.

Be aware that an estimate does not imply accuracy. Information about the globe was limited in the days of Magellan despite the previous exploratory successes by other explorers and merchants. Once Magellan and his crew passed through the strait, everyone entered the unknown by crossing the Pacific Ocean to the Spice Islands. No one knew how long exactly the expedition would take nor that they would face a limited quantity of provisions. Unlike Magellan who kept his eye on the objectives, the others seemed more concerned with keeping themselves alive. In other words, everyone else's head was looking down while he was looking ahead while traversing the unknown. Magellan, who so often in the past had dealt with the unknown, demonstrated the need for patience when progress appeared nebulous at best.

Be flexible in the pursuit of the goal. Magellan's resolve was a positive feature of his personality; however, it was also a liability. He was at times inflexible, even upon receiving realistic suggestions from his immediate reports. When he held his council after discovering the strait, he appeared to have already made up his mind despite most of his direct reports expressing the practicality of returning to Spain. He also failed to listen to his men when he decided to resolve the internal conflict within the Philippines, resulting in his demise.

Prepare to make unpopular decisions. Related to the last point, Magellan had no problem making unpopular decisions, even if it resulted in insubordination by his direct reports and mutiny among crew members. In fact, his resolve seemed to increase in the presence of insubordination and mutiny, which proved to be the right decision. He knew that tolerating such behavior would only increase negative behavior and jeopardize achieving any of the goals set for the expedition. In other words, he expected pushback and was prepared to deal with it accordingly.

Be aware of one's own personality faults that can degrade situational awareness when pursuing a goal. Magellan's arrogance occasionally interfered with his judgment. Despite warnings from his crew, he decided to participate in the struggle between the leaders of Cebu and Mactan, letting his arrogance and ignorance overcome him and impair his situational awareness. In the end, it proved tragic for him and his crew.

Recognize multinational groups can become quite challenging. People from different cultures view the world and experience it differently. These differences can result in conflict. Magellan experienced it when many members of the crew did not feel he should be the commander of the fleet since he was not of their nationality, being originally Spanish and then Portuguese. From the perspective of many of the captains and the crew, he was still a foreigner, thereby adding to the tension that existed throughout the expedition.

Final Thoughts

Ferdinand Magellan faced and survived many travails while pursuing a different oceanic route to the Spice Islands. He faced so many obstacles that only a person of his character could succeed. He faced subterfuge by the king of Portugal as he prepared and embarked on his expedition. He faced suspicion and backlash by the members of his crew, even to the point of mutiny. Even when he reached the Spice Islands, he faced hostility from both crew members and natives, resulting in his death. Still, he focused on his goal despite others wanting to give it up.

How many project managers have faced similar circumstances, short of death? Plenty. They are assigned a project in which some or all team members are embittered and hostile, not just toward the project but also toward the project managers. A project may be a new one that people are assigned to or an existing one that has gone awry. Either way, the project manager must accomplish specific goals. Like Magellan, these project managers must display the same determination to overcome obstacles to achieve the goals of the project.

Chapter 5

Marco Polo: Understanding the Customer

Knowing what a customer needs and wants and being able to determine the difference between the two.

Just mention Marco Polo (born and died 1254 and 1324, respectively) and the name conjures up exotic travel. For 23 years, that is exactly what he did when considering the standards of the time. But he did more. The book about his travels was prepared by a ghostwriter named Rustichello da Pisa whom he met in a Genoese prison several years after his return to Venice. Marco's tales in the book were viewed by many as too incredulous to take seriously. It was not until after his death that the book received the serious attention that it deserves. Even today, some skeptics remain, but for most historians, the book is mainly accurate and factual peppered with some incongruities. When one considers that the book was written essentially from memory, what the young Venetian experienced and witnessed is incredible. The skepticism toward the work, *The Description of the World*, now more commonly known as *The Travels of Marco Polo*, may be due to the ethnocentrism of the Europeans that existed at the time. Yet, ironically, the Mongols and many of the peoples they subjugated were considerably more advanced than the Europeans in the 1300s.

DOI: 10.1201/9781003028734-5

Background

Assume that most of the content of *The Travels of Marco Polo* is a reliable source of information. After all, the book has served as a guide for subsequent explorers and mapmakers during later centuries. Christopher Columbus was inspired by the book, using it to justify his reasons for journeying westward to the Indies. The Christian missionaries saw the book as an opportunity to spread the Word, especially after learning that Kublai Khan expressed an interest in the European faith. Cartographers, such as Paolo dal Pozzo Toscanelli, at the time marked on their maps and globes names like Cathay (today China) and Cipangu (now Japan) based in large part from information contained in *The Travels of Marco Polo*.

Before focusing on Marco Polo, understanding the circumstances of the time can help explain why his travels were so important. Italy was a series of independent states competing and fighting with one another; however, many of these states were leaders in trading throughout the Mediterranean; the Venetians were perhaps the most powerful and preeminent of the states, economically and militarily. The Venetian scope included the Middle East and other parts of Europe. The land that remained a mystery to Venetian traders was the Far East; that is, until Marco Polo; his father, Niccolò Polo; and his uncle, Maffeo, returned to Venice. Prior to Mongol complete control over Central and Far Asia, trade was even more dangerous than it was under their reign. Thanks largely to the rule of Kublai Khan, greater stability existed, which provided the opportunity for the Polos to make a dangerous journey to the Far East. During their long trek, which took about three years to get to Cathay and the same time to return to Venice, dangers lurked all around them. Extreme hot and cold climates. Barren and mountainous terrain. Diseases. Predatory animals. Scarce and often poisonous food. Humans, either thieves or murderers or both. Ironically, the fear of Khan instilled the necessary degree of order that would enable trade to occur between Europeans and Mongols.

The Polos were not average Venetians at the time before their great expeditions to the Far East. They were members of the Venetian nobility and wealthy. The family had made much of its wealth trading with Dalmatia and Constantinople. Niccolò and Maffeo departed for their first trip to the Far East in 1253 along what would centuries later be called the Silk Road; Marco was born shortly thereafter and did not see his father and uncle until the men returned about 15 years later. Both men eventually made it to the court of Khan in Cambulac, known today as Beijing.

Situation

Khan was no stranger to meeting with different peoples like the two Venetians. After all, his court consisted of different religious and ethnic groups, which included Muslims, Persians, Jews, and Chinese. The meeting progressed amiably and both parties seemed receptive toward one another. What was interesting was that Khan expressed an interest in the Italian Peninsula, as well as Christianity, and wanted to use the two Venetians as liaisons with the pope. Khan had a strong interest in religion and exhibited considerable tolerance for all religions throughout the Mongol kingdom. Khan wanted Niccolò and Maffeo to return to Venice to address two requests. He wanted them to bring to him oil from the Holy Sepulchre in Jerusalem. He also wanted 100 priests to return with them. Perhaps the Khan's most important reason for these requests was that he wanted to encourage greater commerce between the Europeans and Mongols. He wanted to leverage his commercial weight, knowing that Europeans wanted goods, such as gems, precious metals, and silk in exchange for what he wanted. While Marco Polo would be credited with being a vehicle for encouraging trade between Europe and Asia, it was, in many respects, Niccolò and Maffeo who laid the groundwork.

Nevertheless, a lucrative business opportunity was just what the two Venetians sought, and it was up to them to make it happen. They began the long tortuous journey back to Venice, protected by a golden passport, known as a paiza, from Kublai Khan and eventually capitalized on their relationship with Pope Gregory X, the successor to Pope Clement IV.

The Polo brothers returned safely to Venice, seeing Marco for the first time as a teenager. In 1271, the Polo brothers were ready to return to Kublai Khan, only this time with Marco. Fortunately, he had two mentors, his father and uncle, who had a wealth of knowledge and experience as it related to traveling the long route to China and negotiating commercial agreements. He would learn even more along the way.

The challenge, of course, was getting 100 priests, especially during the transition between two popes. Arriving at Acre, via a Venetian vessel, they were later able to obtain oil from the Holy Sepulchre. The only challenge now was how to get the 100 priests; instead, the new pope gave them two priests. The dangers inherent in the travel persuaded the two priests to leave the Polos.

Expedition

The expedition was not easy, but it was a significant one during Marco's formative years, exposing him to a world that few other Europeans had previously experienced. Marco learned about different cultures, including their religions, ethnicities, and physical mores, just to name a few. He would endure physical hardships, such as becoming ill in Badakhshan, and life-threatening experiences with assassins high on hashish. In the end, he began to alter his ethnocentric view of the world and embrace a new one. In modern terms, he might be said to have "gone native."

Marco traveled to Armenia, Georgia, Iraq, Persia, Afghanistan, Terak Pass, Pamir mountain region, Taklamakan and Lop deserts, and a host of cities and towns like Tabriz, Sapurgan, Tunocain, Balkh, Khotan, and Ciarcian. This was just an abbreviated list. The main point is that Marco Polo was exposed to a diversified humanity, thanks to Pax Mongolia. Not only did he rattle his preconceptions about the world, he sharpened his skills as an observer, which, just as importantly, enabled him to see the world differently. True, he recognized the commercial value of the carpets from Armenia, the pearls of Tabriz, Muslin fabric of Mosul, salt in Taican, the glandular secretions of the musk deer as perfume and an aphrodisiac, and, of course, silk and gems from China. But he also sharpened his knowledge and observations about the different cultures he encountered. The pervasiveness of Buddhism, along with the presence of other religions, including Islam, Hinduism, and Christianity; the varied sexual behaviors and relationships with wives; the excessive drinking; and the different foods all had an impact on him. But what would impress him the most was the grandeur of the Mongol Empire and its emperor, Kublai Khan. The travels to Cambulac prepared him for what awaited. He was learning to adapt physically and culturally, understanding the complexities of a multicultural, multireligious, and multilingual world and becoming an acute observer without being intrusive. Also along the way, he witnessed the ferocious power of the Mongols, such as their destruction of irrigation systems in Afghanistan.

Marco Polo's skills of observation served him well while serving Kublai Khan. One of the major contributions of *The Travels of Marco Polo* is his detailed descriptions of the Mongols in general and Kublai Khan in particular. His observational powers of the Mongols from a cultural and religious perspective were quite accurate according to historians. What was just as important were the observations about Kublai Khan, his family, and his court. He described his physical characteristics but, just as importantly, revealed his thinking about topics like religion. For example, Marco Polo described his thoughts about religious tolerance, which were quite different from European thinking at the time. The Venetian described in detail the roles and relationships of the members of the court, such as Khan's wife, Chabi, and the intrigues of his Muslim financial administrators, such as Ahmad, who sought power to challenge the Yuan dynasty but failed. His observational details were so keen that he became involved in court activities without being intrusive, becoming a member of Kublai Khan's privy council. Marco's observational powers were impressive, indeed, considering the level of descriptive detail he presented in *The Travels of Marco Polo*.

He exhibited the same observational powers when describing the Mongols. He described their religious beliefs, customs, relationships with other ethnicities, attitudes toward family roles, use of paper currency, sexual activities, calendaring, festivities, diet, and military life, strategies, and tactics. He also developed a facility for several languages, at least four, spoken throughout the empire, which helped him become a trusted emissary of Kublai Khan. He also vividly described major cities like Cambulac and Quinsai (today Hangzhou). Particularly interesting was his description of the Mongol relationships with the Chinese, which managed, for the most part, to maintain peace.

Marco Polo's success with the Mongols was his ability to immerse himself into the culture of the Mongols, known as cultural adaptation. Despite being from Europe and of Caucasian descent, he managed to earn the confidence of Kublai Khan and many of the emperor's followers. In *The Travels of Marco Polo*, the Venetian also kept his ego out of the political fray occurring in the court while at the same time operating in the service of the Khan.

His powers of observation and perception proved valuable in another context. Kublai Khan sent the Venetian to the far reaches of the empire to collect taxes, such as on salt and grain. His observations were poignant on the journey, too, while traveling through western and southeastern parts of China, India, Ceylon, Tibet, Myanmar, Vietnam, Indonesia, and Zanzibar. In many of these areas, he witnessed the powerful destructiveness of the Mongols, such as in Tibet. He also increased his knowledge and interest in Buddhism. Of course, he described the customs, industries, different religions, relationship between the Mongols with the local populace, sexual attitudes, wildlife, agricultural practices, and internal political conflict. He also described an island that would haunt Kublai Khan for his failure to conquer it and would hinder Marco Polo's credibility: Cipangu (Japan). His descriptions of Cipangu would rival the ones for Hangzhou and Camulac, even though no proof exists that he went to Japan. In fact, his descriptions for a few places seemed so incredulous that questions arose whether he visited some of the places. Whether he visited them is not the issue. He demonstrated an ability to listen to people who provided him with the necessary information, which was retained by his gifted memory for details. Most historians agree that these insights in *The Travels of Marco Polo* are accurate.

The Polos' departure from the Mongols was as exciting as their arrival. Kublai Khan needed to send a protected escort for a successor to Queen Bolgana to King Argon of Persia, whose wife had died. As a display of trust Kublai Khan had in Marco Polo, he sent the Venetian, his father, and uncle to King Argon with a flotilla of 13 ships filled with sailors and gifts and a large entourage, along with, of course, the princess and King Argon's three barons. They departed from Quanzhou, then Sumatra, and southern India. A turbulent storm, pirates, and disease wreaked havoc on the fleet and resulted in many deaths, but at least spared a small number of lives, including the Polos and Princess Cocachin. Unfortunately, King Argon had died, and rulership was under a young Quiacatu. The Polos then managed to depart Persia, reaching Trebizond and then Constantinople, Negrepont, and, ultimately, returning to Venice.

Lessons

So, what are some of the key lessons (Figure 5.1) to take away from Marco Polo's experience as it relates to dealing with customers and suppliers?

The Lessons of Marco Polo

- Identify the key stakeholders and understand their relationships
- Listen and observe
- Learn as much as possible about stakeholders by understanding their needs and wants
- Communicate with stakeholders using their language
- Be flexible when dealing with people
- Avoid being blind to a person's shortcomings and your own

Figure 5.1   The Lessons of Marco Polo.

Identify the key stakeholders and understand their relationships. Marco Polo had the unique ability to identify the major parties within an organization, in this case in the court of Kublai Khan. He understood the hierarchy, their roles and responsibilities, their interests, and the explicit and tacit power plays that were happening in the court and even in the other regions of the empire while being self-effacing. He built relationships with many of them without becoming entangled in the internal politics. The Venetian realized that if he became entangled in the internal politics, then he would become a target despite already under suspicion for being a foreigner. If he had taken any action other than that requested by Kublai Khan, he would have become immersed in the internal politics, used as a scapegoat, or even killed.

Listen and observe. Marco Polo knew, at such a young age, the wisdom of listening and observing. Both skills played an important part in his understanding not only Kublai Khan but also Mongolia and its subjugated cultures. In *The Travels of Marco Polo*, he appears to divorce himself in the circumstances and events of the Mongolian Empire. This ability to listen and observe contributed to gaining the confidence of Kublai Khan. True, his excitement comes through in *The Travels of Marco Polo* but does not come across in a way that is judgmental. His earlier descriptions while traveling to Cambulac did come across as judgmental as they relate to sexuality and other religious practices. However, these judgments faded into the background and he seem to embrace the Mongolian attitude toward other religions, such as Buddhism. Even though Marco Polo did not travel to all the places, such as Japan, described in *The Travels of Marco Polo*, he listened to people with whom he had confidence, which enabled him to provide accurate detail.

Learn as much as possible about stakeholders by understanding their needs and wants. The Venetian may have learned the value of understanding from Niccolò and Maffeo as merchants to determine the needs and wants of every customer. Marco Polo clearly realized the most important person he had to please, of course, was Kublai Khan. The ruler placed his trust to such an extent that he appointed him as his emissary to collect taxes throughout the empire. He also trusted him enough (an argument could be made too much) to escort Princess Cocachin to Persia to marry King Argon. Kublai Khan also knew that he could tell information to Marco that others in his court would leak.

Communicate with stakeholders using their language. Marco Polo had the envious ability to learn and speak languages other than his original tongue. He may have spoken Persian, Arabic, Chinese, and Mongolian. He may have picked up one or more Chinese dialects or even Turkish. Regardless of the languages spoken, the point is that this facility to speak the languages understood by the main members of the empire enabled him not only to gain the confidence of Kublai Khan but also to collect and absorb information from people. In turn, he could not only provide "intelligence" to the Mongolian emperor but also the source material for *The Travels of Marco Polo*. Speaking from an important stakeholder's perspective allows for greater understanding and builds confidence.

Be flexible when dealing with people. Knowing a person's needs and wants is not enough. The ability to respond to needs and wants is just as, if not more, important. Kublai Khan recognized that Marco used such abilities and skills to further his own ends. While he often acted with considerable resolve and confidence, the Mongolian leader exhibited mercurial decision-making at times. This situation was the case when dealing with the Song dynasty, which often challenged his authority, in Hangzhou. Marco Polo allowed himself in this circumstance to be of service to Kublai Khan.

Avoid being blind to a person's shortcomings and your own. Marco Polo had one shortcoming. He was blinded by his admiration, perhaps infatuation, with the Mongolian leader. His descriptions often reflected a man of great wisdom and religious tolerance and nothing else to the contrary. Over time, however, the Venetian began to see the ruler's shortcomings. It was not until he witnessed the ruthless suppression of challenges to the authority of the emperor's power, the ruler's declining health, and the subjugation of peoples when resisting membership in the Mongolian Empire did Marco Polo have a realistic portrayal of Kublai Khan. This realization especially showed itself when he joined in with Niccolò and Maffeo to escort the princess to King Argon. All three recognized that Kublai Khan's time as emperor was closing and that a power struggle would follow, which is usually the case under one-man rule. They knew the time was right to return to Venice after fulfilling the Khan's final wishes.

Final Thoughts

Marco Polo was a young man who acquired a once-in-a-lifetime experience on an expedition to the Far East that even today is rare. Under the initial guidance of his father and uncle, he traveled into a world that few understood. He learned about the varied customs, religions, practices, and beliefs of many people, exposing him to a world that few understood. He recognized that not all people thought or lived the same way. Just as remarkable, he learned the importance of communicating with people in their language and understanding their needs and wants, whether in the service of Kublai Khan or when he visited other places in the Mongol Empire.

Project managers can learn much from Marco Polo, who put customers first, spoke to them in their language, and understood their needs and wants. Many project managers, especially technical ones, often communicate with customers using jargon. This type of communication often results in miscommunication. They would better serve themselves and their customers if they tried to speak in the latter's language to understand their needs and wants. The same goes for project managers regarding other stakeholders on their projects. Marco Polo tried to understand and speak the language of other ethnicities within the Mongol Empire and did so successfully.

Chapter 6

Roald Amundsen: Planning

Building a road map to achieve a goal and identifying and obtaining the necessary resource for success.

The wind whips a human body at 50 to 75 miles per hour in blizzard conditions. The snow and ground are indistinct, making it impossible to determine whether a person is going in the right direction. All sense of proportionality also disappears. Parts of the skin begin to flake off, especially on the hands and feet, thanks to frostbite that can eventually result in losing a limb. When the blizzard subsides and the sun creaks through the heavy gray clouds, the sunlight becomes so bright it can cause temporary and, in some cases, permanent blindness. Then the blizzards and whiteouts return, only this time crevasses are seemingly everywhere, endangering men and the dogs that are pulling the sledges; one misstep and men and dogs fall into a bottomless pit. The distances seem longer but the mileage gained gets shorter because of the weariness that consumes man and dog. Tempers rise and a man loses all sense of rationality while others collapse from exhaustion. Then the leader of the expedition must decide whether to proceed, return to base camp, or settle at the current location and continue on the next day—that is, if the men don't fall into a deep sleep and never wake.

Such are the challenges Arctic and Antarctic explorers faced on their expeditions. Going on these expeditions required considerable planning. Most historians agree that the master planner of such expeditions was Roald Amundsen.

DOI: 10.1201/9781003028734-6

Background

Roald Amundsen, born in 1872 and died 1928, was raised in a wealthy family of shipbuilders. He seemed destined for a profession in medicine, as per the wishes of his mother. When his mother passed away, Amundsen decided to pursue a different fate, one as an explorer.

Amundsen gained initial fame for being the first to traverse the Northwest Passage. He then prepared to be the first to reach the North Pole but was eclipsed by Captain Robert Peary, an American, which then led Amundsen to pursue his famous expedition to the South Pole. This time he was trying to beat another captain, Robert Scott.

Perhaps the most formative of his prior experiences was his involvement as first mate in the 1897 Belgica Expedition led by the explorer Belgian Adrien de Gerlache. This expedition traveled to Antarctica with the goal of making astronomical observations. The expedition could have had disastrous consequences if not for the leadership and guidance of two men: Dr. Frederick Cook and Amundsen. The other officers and men became sick; just short of 100 percent of the crew came down with scurvy. Thanks to both men, the crew recovered by eating fresh seal meat. This situation enhanced Amundsen's understanding and cure of scurvy on his future expedition to Antarctica, but he also learned another lesson.

What Amundsen learned was an affirmation of his existing knowledge of the failed British expedition of John Franklin. The lesson was that no expedition can serve two masters; that is, one person must have overall command of the expedition. He noted that conflict often existed between the commander of the expedition and the captain of the ship. In other words, Amundsen recognized the importance of unity of command.

The Belgica expedition taught Amundsen lessons; however, one other experience, prepared him for his future Antarctic expedition: traversing Northwest Passage. In 1905, he embarked on the expedition, making him the first person, along with six other men, to do so successfully with a boat, the *Gjøa*, which he purchased from the famed Fridtjof Nansen who had crossed Greenland. Amundsen followed the route taken by John Franklin. Unlike Franklin, though, Amundsen decided to go "lean and mean." He carried minimal provisions and relied also on hunting. He also learned winter survival from the Intuits and justified the expedition by using scientific investigations, like magnetic observations. Again, he applied these lessons during his Antarctic expedition.

So, what type of person was Amundsen? He was no doubt exceptional. Some of his personal qualities play an instrumental role in planning and executing his famous expedition. Some of his noted qualities include being ambitious, determined, and focused, probably because he set a goal and pursued it regardless of circumstances. He was also a risk-taker, but not a foolish one; he planned in considerable detail each expedition, anticipating the risks that might occur. He also learned from other people and his own experiences when they pertained to his goal, whether exploring the Arctic or Antarctic. He also had his alleged shortcomings. Some accused him of being autocratic, intolerant, and inflexible, especially when dealing with disagreements according to members of his expeditions. He was also seen as secretive, even aloof. As discussed soon, some of these latter observations may have merit. He was always looking for financing for his expeditions and sometimes departed on his expeditions to evade his creditors. He also did not always communicate his intentions to his crew until the last moment; for that matter, he did not even communicate to his most avid supporters like Nansen and the King of Norway.

Situation

The most famous of his expeditions was, of course, to Antarctica. Like his other expeditions, he did his homework; his decisions did not occur on a whim. Amundsen's plans clearly capitalized on his experience from both the Belgica and Northwest Passage expeditions. His well-rounded experience in navigating on land and sea in the Arctic and Antarctica enabled him to develop comprehensive, effective plans. They also reflected his knowledge and experience of people like Dr. Frederick Cook and Fridtjof Nansen.

Despite his extensive planning, most of it must have been principally done by himself, especially when going to Antarctica. He did not reveal the true destination to the crew until he arrived at the Madeira Islands; rather than heading to the Arctic, the destination was going to Antarctica. Not even Nansen or the king knew of the change of plans. Not telling Nansen was surprising since he was using Nansen's boat, the *Fram*. The driving force for the change of destination was Captain Robert Peary's discovery of the North Pole. Interestingly, Amundsen must have had this in the back of his mind prior to arriving at the Madeira Islands to develop the extensive planning details, since significant differences exist between the Arctic and Antarctic environments. Nonetheless, Amundsen offered to pay for the return trip to Norway for anyone on the crew who did not want to continue onward; no one wanted to quit the expedition.

During his planning, Amundsen knew about some of Captain Scott's details for the British expedition. He knew that Scott planned to use ponies; mechanical sledges, and a different breed of huskies. He also knew the route taken by the captain was not the optimum one to take. In the end, Amundsen turned out correct in his insights.

Expedition

Amundsen decided to take a route across the southern continent that was unfamiliar to him. He arrived at the Ross Barrier via the Bay of Whales. When the

Fram arrived close to the Ross Barrier, several men disembarked and then the vessel returned to Buenos Aires. The vessel was to pick up Amundsen and the rest of the men upon their return from the South Pole.

The Norwegian explorer was, however, not totally ignorant of the conditions of the Ross Barrier. He had reviewed maps and other materials about the Ross Barrier and was aware of Ernest Shackleton's previous experience at the location. He was concerned about the danger of calving, which he considered when establishing the base camp, called Framheim.

From the Ross Barrier, the plan was for the team to reach the Queen Maud Range, ascend the Axel Heiberg Glacier, and proceed to the South Pole. Amundsen eventually set up camp at the South Pole for three days and named it Polheim. Like all his other plans, they were calculative, simplistic, and direct.

One aspect of the plan that helped to overcome the danger of getting lost was establishing three depots and several caches of provisions along the route to the South Pole; depots were established at the following latitudes: 80 degrees south, 81 degrees, and 82 degrees. The depots and caches helped the team as they progressed toward the South Pole and when they returned to Framheim. The depots and caches were well-provisioned.

Establishing depots and caches was not easy due to the potential danger of becoming lost. Fog and snow plagued the team from the beginning. The weather was unstable, causing delays because it shifted from warm to cold and vice versa. To help in determining their return, the team placed bamboo poles with flags at every tenth-mile interval and placed dried fish at much shorter intervals; the smell of the fish served as a beacon for the huskies taking the team back to Framheim after establishing the depots and caches.

The entire expedition was well-provisioned. Amundsen calculated the number of calories required daily for each man and provided the men with food that met the requirements; these foods included seal meat, dried fish, biscuits, chocolate, pemmican, and margarine. He even calculated the quantity of meat provided by the carcass of each dog. Amundsen also calculated the calories needed by each man while traversing to and from the South Pole and provided them with adequate levels of pemmican and other foods.

As mentioned earlier, Amundsen believed in being lean and mean. For example, he brought approximately 100 huskies with the idea that they would not only pull the sledges but also become food during the travel to and from the South Pole.

The crew was also small by design. He would subdivide the team into two groups, or teams: the sea and land parties. Responsibilities were assigned to each man, and some of them were responsible for their sledges and the dogs that pulled them. The number of men in the final pursuit of the South Pole was also small; only four men, four sledges, and 52 dogs, eventually butchering many of them.

Despite the planning, the expedition faced several risks.

One risk was the impact of extreme cold. The temperatures often fell to minus 50 degrees Fahrenheit or more. The temperatures were brutal on men, causing the team to retreat due to frostbite. The huskies also found it difficult to function in the extreme cold. The team realized this shock of the weather when establishing the depots and caches.

Another risk was getting lost. Sometimes Amundsen found it difficult to determine the direction to proceed due to the combination of winds and blizzards. Sometimes, the meters on the sledges and compasses failed to work and visibility inhibited performing any dead reckoning. Even astronomical observations were difficult at times. The sighting of bamboo poles every tenth mile helped to keep them on the right path. They also built six-foot towers at specific intervals along the way to the South Pole, which served to guide them back to Framheim. When weather permitted, they used two mountains to guide their approach to the Axel Heiberg Glacier: Mount Nansen and Mount Don Pedro Christophersen.

Still another risk was slow progress, which meant, potentially, the team might not be the first to reach the South Pole. Crevasses were an impediment. Indeed, one of the sledges was almost lost in a hole due to blizzard conditions. If the crevasses did not pose enough of a challenge, hardened snow with drifting snow, known as sastrugi, made it difficult for the dogs to pull the sledges. Both conditions slowed progress toward the South Pole.

A major risk was insubordination by a member of the team. Amundsen had learned from previous experiences and from his readings of other explorers that challenges to command could result in an expedition's failure. This risk was one of his major concerns. Under one instance, such a challenge surfaced by one of the members of the team, and Amundsen quickly dealt with it by pulling the individual from the team going to the South Pole and restricting him to Framheim. Amundsen knew that the long winters could lead to boredom and trouble among the team members and other incidences of challenges to his authority. He had the men spend their time making improvements to sledges and harnesses, as well as redistributing weight among the sledges and provided moments of entertainment.

Another major risk was running out of food. He believed that a major reason why Scott and Shackleton on earlier expeditions failed to reach the South Pole was due to a lack of food. Amundsen was determined not to allow that to happen by planning food requirements in detail. He ensured that no significant shortage of food occurred and that no one came down with scurvy.

As Amundsen and his team continued toward the direction of the South Pole, the weather improved, and he was able to determine their location through solar observations and calculate the remaining distance to the South Pole. Amundsen reached the South Pole on December 14, 1911, planted the Norwegian national flag, pitched a tent, left a letter for Scott, and named the location Polheim. The team remained in the location for three days to perform calculations to ensure that they were, indeed, at the South Pole. Thanks in part to outstanding planning, Amundsen had beat Scott by a little over a month.

Lessons

So, what are some of the key lessons (Figure 6.1) project managers can learn from Roald Amundsen's experience planning an expedition.

Plan to prepare yourself. The Norwegian explorer did not become an explorer overnight. He prepared himself for the great achievement that followed; he also learned during his expeditions, and he learned from the experiences of others, such as Dr. Frederick Cooper, Ernest Shackleton, Captain Robert Scott, and Fridtjof Nansen. Just as importantly, he learned from his own experiences, such as on the Belgica and Northwest Passage expeditions. He also took training on seamanship. He used this knowledge and experience to prepare comprehensive plans which enabled him to execute efficiently and effectively his expedition to the South Pole.

Determine the path in advance. Amundsen used his goal of reaching the South Pole as a basis for his planning. He determined the route to take that logically seemed clear and simple. He then identified all the activities he would have to perform before the expedition began, leaving nothing to chance. He determined the vessel, crew members, route, and provisions. In a sense, he also knew the time line, the climatic conditions, and the need to reach the South Pole before Scott. Although he "miscommunicated" to Nansen and the king his real goal, his complete reversal of direction indicated his planning was flexible enough to modify the goal at the last minute while in the Madeira Islands.

Verify the plan is on track. Once the team reached the Bay of Whales and established Framheim, Amundsen knew he had to find a way to determine his performance in achieving his goal. When he laid the poles on the way to establish the depots and placed dried fish every quarter mile so the dogs could return them to Framheim, he recognized the necessity of keeping on track, even when considering the distance. He also recognized the need for the crew to help themselves return from the South Pole by building a number of six-foot towers every nine miles, which served as directional finders and checkpoint reviews. On the way to the South Pole, he used meters, compasses, dead reckoning, and solar measurements to

The Lessons of Roald Amundsen

- Plan to prepare yourself
- Determine the path in advance
- Verify the plan is on track
- Determine provisions and logistical requirements
- Identify roles and responsibilities
- Recognize the importance of unity of command

Figure 6.1   The Lessons of Roald Amundsen.

determine progress and remaining distance. He was also conscious of his milestone to reach the South Pole before Scott.

Determine provisions and logistical requirements. Amundsen realized the importance of ensuring that the expedition was provisioned with ample food and supplies. He carefully selected and calculated the quantity of the food, from biscuits to huskies, to maintain the strength of the men. He also recognized the potential for his team to experience the horror of scurvy, which he especially understood after what he experienced during the Belgica expedition. Establishing depots and caches further reflected the necessity of ensuring that the men were supplied with food and establishing "logistical warehouses." The depots also served as a haven for the men to recover from the grueling environmental conditions.

Identify roles and responsibilities. Amundsen recognized the need for every man to know his roles and responsibilities. He defined roles and responsibilities starting with himself at the top as the expedition leader. As noted earlier, he also broke the team into sea and land teams, each with distinct goals and roles. He then further assigned activities to each of the men; for example, he assigned responsibilities, such as cooking, carpentry, and charting. Assignments included giving four men the responsibility of a sledge and six huskies each.

Recognize the importance of unity of command. The Norwegian explorer valued the concept of unity of command. He had learned from his knowledge about his hero Captain John Franklin and other readings that the commander of an expedition and the captain of a vessel could be at odds with one another. He also witnessed it during the Belgica expedition. When the incident occurred where one of his former subordinates questioned his expertise and behavior, Amundsen responded, although a few critics felt, harshly. One wonders if Amundsen had died on the expedition, however, would the expedition continue due to his autocratic and secretive style.

Final Thoughts

Roald Amundsen did not just talk about planning; he demonstrated its importance before and during his expedition to Antarctica. He knew from previous experiences that if he wanted to be the first to reach the South Pole, he would need to plan. He used the wisdom, knowledge, and experiences of others and his own to develop a plan that was realistic, not a product of fantasy. He calculated reliable estimates for resources from manpower to food for his men, assigned responsibilities, determined the path to follow, established benchmarks, and identified risks. His plans were lean and mean because they were realistic and possibly because he did not have access to many financial resources. The only problem with his approach was that he was so secretive and practically autocratic in his approach that few really understood his plans, and he reluctantly shared them at the last minute in the Canary Islands.

Most project managers realize the importance of planning. The challenge they face is that the vision and goals for their projects are not well-defined, as Amundsen's were. Hence, their plans are often vague. Resource estimates are unrealistic, roles and responsibilities ill-defined, and the milestones impractical. Some plans lack buy-in from key stakeholders, a shortcoming in Amundsen's plans. Many project managers today, unlike Amundsen, do not have the luxury of picking their own team members and the financial resources to achieve the vision and goals of their projects. Still, they can learn much from Amundsen's experience in planning for a project.

Chapter 7

James Cook: Integrating

Ensuring all elements of an organization perform together efficiently and effectively.

Mention the word "explorer" and the name that comes to mind right away for most people is James Cook. His life has inspired television shows, movies, and poses as a standard from which to judge all expeditions. While some of his actions have been construed as controversial under contemporary times, historians generally have put a positive perspective on his accomplishments. Only one explorer has been viewed as positively as Cook, the Chinese explorer Zheng He. Cook's explorations were mostly one of peace and learning, which, ironically, led to a tragic and violent ending.

Background

What is quite remarkable, however, is the man himself. He epitomized the Horatio Alger storyline of British society. Born in 1728, he came from what would be considered a poor family background of little consequence. His father was a Scottish farm laborer and his mother a villager. Undeterred, he became a self-learner, which was the only educational option available for a young man of his stature in those days. After receiving the kindness of a village woman who taught him how to read, he attended a small school that covered the basics. Cook desired to enhance his learning, teaching himself mathematics, which helped him to become a premier navigator. After working as an apprentice, he went to the city of Whitby, which was a center for coal shipping. Through hard work, he made a name for himself as a competent seaman to the point that he was offered command of a collier. However, Cook obviously desired something more; he joined the British navy as an ordinary

DOI: 10.1201/9781003028734-7

seaman, which began a long career of progression up the naval hierarchy. Prior to the Seven Years' War, he was promoted to master's mate, and when the conflict arrived, he reached the position of master during the siege of St. Louisburg in Nova Scotia and the capture of Quebec. An interesting story is that Cook encountered an artillery officer who taught him, a quick study, to make a map of a harbor. To what extent the knowledge he acquired helped further his upward climb no one knows. Nevertheless, he must have applied what he learned when he served on the HMS *Pembroke* and mapped the shore of Nova Scotia, Newfoundland, and the St. Lawrence River, receiving accolades from his senior leadership.

Success often comes, though, at a cost. Cook returned to England and married Elizabeth Batts and then received orders to return to Canada to apply his reputable skills in mapmaking. (As a side note, his maps were of such quality that some are still used). Upon returning to London, his work not only impressed the Admiralty but also the Royal Society. One achievement during this period was not just surveying the coast of Newfoundland but also observing the eclipse of the sun; the results so impressed the Royal Society that it helped lay the groundswell for his first expedition, observing the transit of Venus.

Before discussing the first expedition, one should get a glimpse of the personality that made up James Cook. The captain had several of the qualities that many great naval men possessed. He had considerable resolve in achieving his goals. Not surprisingly, this required having great self-confidence. In addition to being a superb navigator, he had one quality that was even rarer among other commanders: he listened when circumstances required him to do so. Still, he was a disciplinarian who ran a tight ship while at sea, even though on land his control appeared to slacken at times. He had a curious mind; Cook tried to learn the customs of the people he ran across as he traveled the globe, as well as support the efforts of the scientists he had on board. Cook was not, of course, perfect. He had two flaws in his personality, which, under certain circumstances, were assets and in other situations were liabilities. He was impatient and hot-tempered, which especially surfaced on the third expedition.

Situation

England around the mid-1700s ruled the waves, albeit not totally; other countries explored the globe, like France and Spain. However, France was trying to recover financially from the French and Indian War, which did not end until 1763. Spain focused on its existing territories, such as the west coast of North America. The Pacific coast remained largely unexplored. Within England, the relationship between the Royal Society and the Admiralty had developed a symbiotic relationship, with the former pushing for greater scientific discovery and the latter playing a significant role in spreading the British flag. One area of the globe that was largely unexplored and caught the interest of the British was the Pacific Ocean.

Very few men had the qualifications to lead an expedition of scientific discovery, spread the British flag, and apply navigational expertise to the vastly unexplored Pacific Ocean; James Cook was one of those men.

First Expedition

The major goal of the first expedition was to go to Tahiti to observe the transit of Venus in early June 1769. Cook, now a lieutenant, had a few other goals to accomplish, some planned and others emergent. Before leaving Plymouth, England, he had to prepare the HMS *Endeavor*, a converted collier, for the long voyage. One of the major preparations was to ensure that the crew could survive the dreaded curse of scurvy by stocking the vessel with animals, as well as vegetables and fruit, most famously sauerkraut. He had considerable success eliminating scurvy, thanks also in part to keeping the decks clean with vinegar and ensuring the good personal hygiene of the crew. He could not, unfortunately, overcome death among his crew; several men died from malaria and dysentery upon the return voyage to London; he had lost about 30 percent of his men.

The expedition was a tremendous success. He observed the transit of Venus, making accurate calculations. Just as importantly, Cook had accomplished something else that is not often appreciated. He had learned about and respected the culture of the peoples that he had engaged. He became familiar with the customs and behaviors of the Tahitians, which would prove invaluable during the remainder of the expedition. He also did not allow his crew to exhibit disrespect toward the native population, even to the point, which he did sparingly, of flogging members of his crew. His bringing on board a Tahitian chief, Tupia, and his son proved invaluable when dealing with other Polynesians, particularly in New Zealand. Another accomplishment was creating detailed, reliable maps.

Though he did not disprove the legendary continent known as Terra Australis Incognita, he came close and would lead another expedition to address that issue. He successfully explored the coast of New Zealand and the strait between the North and South Islands; he confirmed that New Zealand was not part of a continent, as well as encountered the Maoris. His encounters with the Maoris could have turned negative, but Cook was determined to respect the natives. Using the interpretive skills of Tupia, he was able to bridge some of the differences between them and the English so much so that members of his crew were able to intermingle with the Maoris for several days and nights. The perceived "thieving" of the Maoris on the vessel strained the relationship, as they sought iron objects, which proved a persistent problem for Cook on all his expeditions. At one point, a few Maoris tried to seize Tupia's son, but the crew was able to save him after firing at their canoe.

From New Zealand, he proceeded to what is today called Tasmania (originally Van Diemen's Land) but the weather did not help his journey. He then followed the east coast of Australia, which was known as New Holland, and entered the legendary Botany Bay where he encountered the Aborigines, and the scientist Joseph Banks collected his specimens.

A frightening incident occurred while sailing around the Great Barrier Reef off Australia. The HMS *Endeavor* struck a coral reef, which threatened to sink the vessel and maroon the crew. Water sucked into the holding area of the vessel. In a desperate attempt to preclude sinking, the crew tossed heavy items, such as cannons and ballast. However, more was required. Cook, undeterred, heeded the advice of a subordinate and managed to stop the leakage by a combination of manure, a large piece of coral, and a canvas sail. He then was able to buy time to make the necessary repairs.

Before returning to London, Cook proceeded north, after declaring New South Wales for England, and headed to New Guinea, stopping at Batavia. He then returned via the Cape of Good Hope to London in 1771, receiving accolades and a promotion before embarking on his second expedition.

Second Expedition

The second expedition was one of great accomplishments. But unlike the first one, it was somewhat less exciting. Cook, now a commander, had made all the preparations, leveraging his knowledge on maintaining the health of his crew. He paid even more attention to reducing the chance of scurvy affecting the crew. Additionally, he planned to ensure at various points in the expedition that they collect provisions, especially food, such as livestock and fruits in Cape Town and New Zealand. Cook also, unlike the first expedition, had four chronometers, astronomers, and scientists in addition to the crew.

Cook had two vessels under his command: the HMS *Resolution* and HMS *Adventure*. He was the captain of the HMS *Resolution*; Tobias Furneaux was the captain of the HMS *Adventure*. Cook demonstrated his brilliance as a risk manager by planning rendezvous points, such as Dusky Bay in New Zealand if, and they did, both vessels lost one another. This became important since one of the goals of the expedition was to sail past the Antarctic Circle; the weather on the southern continent often hinder visibility.

Captain Cook had traveled more than the first voyage; some estimates put the figure at approximately 70,000 miles. Regardless of the miles, Cook had achieved some notable accomplishments. He became the first ever to cross the Antarctic Circle, traveled there a second time only to be stopped by an ice pack, and conducted a full circumnavigation around a southern latitude. Other accomplishments included mapping the south Pacific, such as Easter Island and the Marquesas Islands; discovering New Caledonia; surveying the area between latitudes 41 and 46 degrees, which had never previously been done; and revisiting Tahiti to end up witnessing a conflict among the natives. After rounding Cape Horn, the discoveries continued, to include South Georgia and South Sandwich Islands, and returning to England in 1775. Often overlooked was an accomplishment of the HMS *Adventure*, which had departed before the HMS *Resolution*, performing the first easterly circumnavigation of the globe.

Upon his return, Cook received wide recognition. The Admiralty promoted him to the position of post-captain, he received the Copley Medal from the Royal Society for his writing on scurvy, and was given a pension and assigned to manage a naval hospital. For a man of action like Cook, retirement must have resembled being sent to pasture. When asked for a recommendation of someone to take a major expedition to find the Northwest Passage from the Pacific side of the North American continent, he picked just the right person: himself.

Third Expedition

In 1776, Captain Cook commanded two ships: the HMS *Resolution* and HMS *Discovery*, with the former under his leadership and the other under Charles Clerke. The major goal was, as just mentioned, to find the Northwest Passage from the Pacific side of the North American continent. However, fate had other plans for Cook, Clerke, and their crews.

The vessels rounded the Cape of Good Hope, replete with livestock and horses, and the expedition proceeded without any major complications toward Australia, Tasmania, and New Zealand until making an intermediate stop at Christmas Island and the Society Islands, specifically Tahiti. From Tahiti, the expedition continued onward to the west coast of North America to pursue the Northwest Passage.

The expedition in search of the Northwest Passage was alone significant. But Cook followed along the west coast of North America with a short stay in what is today the state of Oregon and stopped at Vancouver Island to conduct repairs on the vessels. Then he continued northward through the Bering Strait, crossing over the Polar, or Arctic, Circle until stopped by ice packs. He then followed along the Aleutian chain. During the journey, he conducted charting.

Cook now proceeded toward his fateful trek back to Hawaii, anchoring in Kealakekua Bay near the big island, Hawaii. The reception was magnificent, with Cook exchanging gifts, including pigs and dogs, with the king; the captain receiving feathered cloaks and the king a sword and cloths. The reason is that Cook arrived at a time of a festival for Lono, a legendary god returning. The large canvasses of the ships represented the return of Lono. Cook then departed northwards, only to encounter strong gales that destroyed the main mast of his ship.

Upon his return to Hawaii, the integration of all aspects of his expedition came apart. The Hawaiians were not receptive, in part because of the behavior of the crew toward the women. The provisioning of food to the crew also strained the natives. If that was not enough, members of the crew were accused of desecrating a temple, known as a morai. The English were also getting irritated with the Hawaiians. When they boarded the vessels, Hawaiians stole objects, especially ones made of iron. The thievery exceeded Cook's patience when the natives stole a cutter from the *Discovery*. Now everything began to unravel.

Cook decided he wanted to take the king, named Terreeoboo, hostage and exchange the native for the cutter. The captain came ashore with a small force. Cook encountered the king's two sons, who led the captain to a house in the village of Kowrowa. The king said he knew nothing about the theft of the cutter but agreed to come aboard; Cook changed his mind about taking the king hostage and left. Then the situation deteriorated as Cook worked his way toward the shore.

The captain found himself surrounded by Hawaiians as the marines fell back farther. The Hawaiians heard distant gunfire; the Hawaiians reacted, especially after hearing that a chief had been killed. The natives closed in, and Cook struggled with one of them. Cook fired a small shot followed by a larger one, which killed the Hawaiian. In the end, four marines lay dead, and Cook was clubbed, stabbed, and drowned as the rest of the crew stayed offshore. In about 20 minutes, the whole ordeal was over, ending with the death of one of the world's greatest explorers.

Clerke ordered the firing of the canons from the HMS *Discovery* to cause the Hawaiians to retreat. In the end, only a few bones and ashes were returned to the British, who buried them at sea. The remainder of Cook's belongings on his person were distributed among the Hawaiians. The mast was then brought from the shore and repaired on the HMS *Resolution*. Not long after, Clerke died from consumption, and command was assumed by Lieutenant John Gore, who returned the crew to London in October 1780.

Lessons

So, what are some key lessons (Figure 7.1) project managers can learn from James Cook's experience as an integrator?

Recognize a leader's behavior can have an impact. Integration requires everyone to work together, from the top to the bottom of an organization; it is no different whether a business project or an expedition. For the first and second voyages,

The Lessons of James Cook

- Recognize a leader's behavior can have an impact
- Take a holistic perspective
- Recognize technical expertise is not enough
- Look after the health and welfare of the team
- Focus on the primary goals first
- Adapt to changing circumstances

Figure 7.1 The Lessons of James Cook.

Cook exhibited leadership that won him accolades from the Admiralty to the Royal Society. Then something went awry during the third voyage. Cook's temper and impatience became uncontrollable. As a result, he communicated less with his officers, became more impulsive, and made rash decisions as demonstrated on his return to Hawaii. His impatience and temper resulted not only in his death but also in the deaths of the marines who came ashore with him; all communication and coordination went into disarray. The men were shocked at the loss of their commander, yet the damage had already been done. Some speculation exists that his behavior had deviated so much that he might have suffered a physical ailment that contributed to his behavior.

Take a holistic perspective. One of the outstanding qualities of Captain Cook was his ability to see the big picture of his expeditions. He kept his focus on the goals of the expedition; ensured that his crew was well taken care of, even when they exhibited displeasure; and anticipated how he would engage with people from other cultures. He involved himself in all preparations for an expedition, from planning to execution. His holistic perspective was largely due to his vast experience as a seaman, as well as serving as a junior and senior officer in the British navy.

Recognize technical expertise is not enough. Cook was primarily in the earlier part of his career a navigator and a cartographer. Few people at the time were his equal. He also knew that he had to expand his knowledge and expertise, and he did. He did not limit himself to such a narrow focus, probably because he was a self-learner. Few other explorers took an interest in other cultures and the flora, fauna, and terrain of the areas like he did. When possible, he allowed scientists, like Joseph Banks, to perform their responsibilities. In other words, Cook took a multidisciplinary perspective, saw the big picture, and integrated all activities and components while everything centered on achieving one or more goals.

Look after the health and welfare of the team. Cook respected his crew, even though he was a harsh disciplinarian. He knew that if he had exercised a lack of discipline, the efficient and effective operations of the vessels would decline. He also ensured that the men adhered to the dietary regimen that helped to prevent scurvy. He tried to prevent the infection of venereal disease among his crew despite the challenges in trying to keep his men separate from the female native population, both in the interests of his men and the female natives. Cook knew that a healthy crew meant his vessels could perform efficiently and effectively as a whole. The HMS *Endeavor*, under Captain Clerke, demonstrated that poor discipline and illness could impact the overall performance of a vessel. The HMS *Endeavor* lacked the discipline of the HMS *Resolution* because Clerke was too weak from consumption; a few historians attributed part of the tragedy on the third expedition to this circumstance.

Focus on the primary goals first. Cook did not take his eyes off the goals for each expedition. During the first expedition, for example, he kept his eye on the transit of Venus. During the second expedition, for example, he penetrated the Antarctic Circle and explored the east coast of Australia. During the third expedition, he focused on identifying the Northwest Passage. All three goals, despite the tragedy of the last expedition, were achieved. The goals came first, and then he could take advantage of other opportunities—e.g., identifying, charting, and exploring other islands. In other words, all decisions and actions worked together to achieve the goals. All aspects of the third expedition appeared to occur efficiently and effectively until he returned to Hawaii.

Adapt to changing circumstances. For the first and second expeditions, Cook adapted to different circumstances quite well. When encountering other cultures, such as the Maoris and the Tahitians, he adapted to their customs quite adroitly. When his vessel smashed into the Great Barrier Reef, he took the advice of a subordinate, which resulted in the ship staying afloat and eventually being repaired. Of course, he did not adapt so well to the cannibalistic practices of the natives or their thievery, especially items made of iron. Even then, he was able to maintain forbearance until the third expedition. Adaptability requires understanding the big picture and ensuring that all aspects of the expedition function efficiently and effectively; otherwise, adaptability becomes difficult because one aspect of an expedition may be doing something contrary to what the other part is doing, as demonstrated during the third expedition, thus generating dysfunctional results.

Final Thoughts

James Cook knew how to plan and run an expedition. Much of his knowledge was based on practical experience gained from rising through the ranks of the Royal Navy. The results of his first and second expeditions were a testament to his ability to manage and lead all aspects of an expedition, whether it involved one vessel or many vessels. As a result, he was able to deal with expected and unexpected situations. He was also able to learn and work with all peoples, from members of his crew to the natives he countered. His decisions and plans were based upon the goals for his expedition and seeing the "big picture." But just as remarkable is that he lost very few men because he looked after their health and welfare; scurvy was virtually nonexistent. Even the third voyage was an example of his talent and brilliance; only after he returned to Hawaii did the expedition unravel, which resulted in his death.

Like Cook, project managers need to rise above a technical perspective and see the big picture. All the activities of their projects will achieve better results if they manage and lead them in an integrated manner that focuses on achieving the vision and goals. If they look at the big picture, they can operate more efficiently and effectively. Too often, processes on a project conflict with one another, creating wasted time and effort, as well as causing frustration among team members, mainly because their projects lose focus on the vision and goals. Cook knew the value of integrating based upon a vision and goals; successful project managers do the same.

Chapter 8

Hernán Cortés: Motivating

Providing incentives for a team to meet or exceed expectations regarding performance.

The name Hernán Cortés often generates one of two feelings in a person: admiration or revulsion and, in some cases, both. He represents the power and glory of the Old World and its shock and terror all at the same time. He brought into confrontation, two worldviews that have significant impacts even to this day. Almost 500 years later, the ramifications of his actions and that of his men have set the stage for what exists today throughout the Western Hemisphere.

Hernán Cortés laid waste to a highly evolved native culture using a comparatively small group of men, called mercenaries or conquistadors, to conquer an empire of close to four million people. The Aztecs, under the leadership of Moctezuma II, translated as the Courageous Lord, ruled this empire. He was protected by a cadre of warriors, such as the Eagles and Jaguars, as well as thousands of other fighters, and a priesthood that would soon crumble when confronted with what was perceived as a fulfillment of a prophecy, the return of Quetzalcoatl, translated as the Feathered Serpent. The appearance of Cortés and the timing of his arrival could not be more fortuitous for a man like Cortés who convinced men, ladies, and other Indians to follow him. The Aztec prophecy foretold of a white-skinned man with a beard returning from the east after a long time being forced out of the region. Cortés was prophesized to return during the Aztecan calendar year 1 Reed every 52 years; 1519 was that year.

DOI: 10.1201/9781003028734-8

Background

Moctezuma ruled from the city of Tenochtitlán, translated as the Place of the Prickly Pear Cactus, which had a vast array of buildings, temples, and a large market that could hold 60,000 people. Primary access to the Venetian-like city was via causeways protecting the city from other Indian peoples. As impressive as the city was, Tenochtitlán also was the center of the activity that would play into the hands of Cortés. Human sacrifice to the gods, such as the war god Huitzilopochtli, translated as the Hummingbird on the Left and, Tezcatlipoca, translated as the Mirror That Smokes, was a major religious behavior not only in the city but also throughout the empire. The sacrifices, like just about all religious sacrifices, were made to appease one or more gods to ensure good weather and plentiful crops. These sacrifices played into Cortés's game plan to defeat the Aztecs; such practices led other native peoples, such as the Totonacs and Tlaxcalans, to form an alliance with Cortés.

Cortés did not go on his famous expedition without some understanding of what to expect. He had the benefit of two previously failed expeditions. The first one occurred in 1517, sponsored by the governor of Cuba, Diego Velázquez. The leader of the expedition was Captain Francisco Hernández de Córdoba. By most reckonings, the expedition was a failure after confronting a Mayan civilization at Cape Catoche. Initially, the encounter was cordial but soon turned violent, resulting in the captain returning to Cuba with approximately half of his crew dead. However, Córdoba managed to bring back gold, which was enough to have Velázquez seriously consider another expedition, only this time led by a relative, Juan de Grijalva.

Juan de Grijalva arrived in Cozumel in early 1518. He then landed at the same spot as Córdoba and suffered the same fate. However, unlike the earlier expedition, this one continued, reaching Veracruz only to discover evidence of human sacrifices. He conversed with the Totonacs during a friendly encounter. The Totonacs revealed that a great civilization existed that the natives, like many other ones that Cortés would discover, hated. And, of course, Grijalva probably construed that also meant more gold.

Situation

Meanwhile, back in Cuba was a young man who had made a name for himself, Hernando, or Hernán for short, Cortés. He was originally from the region of Estremadura, a place that seemed to be a tough training ground for future conquistadors like himself. He came from a military family; his father served as a captain with the infantry, but Cortés decided to become a lawyer by attending the University of Salamanca; however, he took a radical turn and wanted to become a warrior like his father who had served in foreign wars in such places as the Italian Peninsula. His expectations did not, however, turn out. In 1506, he left for Cuba, where he became a rancher and eventually made it to Santiago and the government of Cuba, where he became chief magistrate, mayor, and an acquaintance of Velázquez.

Cortés became interested, even financially, in the expeditions of Córdoba and Grijalva; he recognized that their limited progress presented him with opportunities for adventure, riches, and power. Such opportunities could not help but entice a man like Cortés. He was known to be a gambler, a risk-taker who had great resolve in pursuing his goals. He was cool-headed, coupled with the gift of patience to wait for the right opportunity and then strike quickly. Adding to these characteristics of intelligence, cleverness, and luck backed with a technologically superior force; the Aztecs were inevitably slated for trouble.

Expedition

The conquistador took the leap, borrowing money to finance part of the expedition and Velázquez financing the other half. Then the governor appointed Cortés captain-general. Velázquez wanted the expedition to be one of discovery, not mayhem, as it eventually became. Before the departure of Cortés on February 18, 1519, the governor tried to stop the conquistador, realizing he might have made a deal with the devil. Cortés, determined and ruthless as always, decided to continue with the expedition after procuring the necessary resources and offering profit sharing among his fellow Spaniards. Nothing was going to stop him, even if it meant having one of Velázquez's messengers killed.

The expedition was ready for action, consisting of 11 vessels and 530 men, along with over 100 sailors. The expedition's weapons included artillery, cannon, arquebuses, falconets, swords, dogs (such as mastiffs), and horses. The dogs and horses proved useful for generating fear among the Aztecs.

He arrived at Yucatán and then proceeded to Cozumel. Conversing with the natives, he learned about two captives, one of which served as an interpreter; his name was Geronimo de Aguilar. He joined the expedition as a Mayan translator after being a Mayan slave for eight years. The other Spaniard did not join the expedition.

Cortés continued to explore Yucatán, Tabasco River, and Frontera. The engagement with the Indians turned violent, and the Spaniards won the battle but with casualties. The natives of the Tabasco River turned cordial, presenting gifts, food, and women. Here he met a reputedly beautiful woman named Malinche, also known as Malindi and Doña Marina. She spoke Mayan and Nahuatl, the second one being the language of the Aztecs. All three, Cortés, Aguilar, and Malinche would prove invaluable in talking with the different tribes comprising the Aztec Empire. Malinche eventually learned to speak Spanish.

The fleet reached the Isla de Sacrificios, so named because of what the Grijalva expedition witnessed in a temple. The conquistadors entered the Kingdom of

Zempoala, which was a land with several natives, including the Totonacs, discussed earlier regarding the Juan de Grijalva expedition. The encounter with the Totonacs was positive. The natives and the Spaniards exchanged gifts. The Totonacs even accommodated the Spaniards by allowing the expedition to place a cross on top of a pyramid. They also revealed that other natives, such as the Tlaxcalans were hostile toward the Aztecs.

Teudile, a messenger from Moctezuma II, met with Cortés in Veracruz. Teudile and Cortés discussed the Grijalva expedition and what gifts and other hospitality to expect from Moctezuma and exchanged gifts. One delightful gift, at least to the Spaniards, was gold, including a chest full of objects made of the metal. Naturally, the exchange only meant one thing: there was more from where that came from, and Teudile told him so. To top off the exchange, being a showman, Cortés demonstrated his military capability, which frightened Teudile and his entourage. His apparent intent was to have Teudile spread the word of the Spanish military might.

That was exactly what happened. The natives reported to Moctezuma about the power of the Spaniards and that Cortés was Quetzalcoatl. Moctezuma reacted to the event by sending more gifts to Cortés, which only fed the conquistador's determination to continue. However, Cortés may have had another reason to proceed toward Tenochtitlán: Velázquez wanted Cortés to return and be tried. Using his legal background, he outsmarted Velázquez by setting up a municipality called Villa Rica de Vera Cruz and then was elected captain-general of the town. Cortés no longer was under the tutelage of Velázquez but of the king of Spain.

Cortés was also facing potential insurrection within the ranks. Several members of the expedition wanted to take the gold and return to Cuba, even attempting to seize one of the vessels. Cortés also demonstrated his cleverness in another regard; he wrecked his fleet to prevent any notion of returning to Cuba. The fleet was not destroyed and much of it was recoverable enough to create a small flotilla to attack the Aztec city. He also ruthlessly dealt with the insurrectionists, hanging two of them, cutting off the feet of another, and lashing the sailors, thereby sending a signal to his men. The expedition no longer had any choice but to proceed onward to Tenochtitlán.

As the Spaniards continued toward Tenochtitlán, Cortés encountered the Tlaxcalans. Fearful that the Spaniards were in cahoots with the Aztecs, these natives engaged in a violent clash. The Tlaxcalans were unable to defeat the Spaniards and saw Cortés as a god. He recognized the significance of the event was not that the Spaniards defeated the Tlaxcalans, although that was important. Rather, it revealed that the Aztecs were not loved by the other native peoples. Cortés saw this as an opportunity to build useful alliances, starting with the Tlaxcalans. A major source of their friction with the Aztecs were the sacrifices.

With the aid of the Tlaxcalans, Cortés struck the city of Cholula. He massacred thousands of the natives and captured several chiefs and killed them. The event only proved his invincibility as a god. Moctezuma responded with more gifts for

Cortés, which included, of course, gold as a sign of friendship accompanied by a plea, contradictorily, to not continue toward Tenochtitlán.

Cortés with his fellow conquistadors nevertheless worked their way toward Tenochtitlán, passing between the two famous volcanoes, Popocatépetl and Iztaccihautl, and met initially with Aztec chiefs who offered more gifts, again only indicating to Cortés that Moctezuma, the Great Speaker, or tlatoani, was acting out of fear.

On November 8, 1519, the Spaniards and their native allies began their entrance into the city, working their way down a five-mile causeway. Cortés and his fellow conquistadors and Indian allies were decked out in full military regalia; the Spaniards were perched upon their horses to demonstrate their military might. The Aztecs marveled at the grand entrance and the Spaniards were swarmed by people and greeted ceremoniously. The bridge was soon lowered on the causeway, allowing the Spaniards to proceed. Soon, Cortés and Moctezuma greeted one another. The conquistador dismounted and was rebuffed when trying to embrace the Aztec leader. Moctezuma then showered Cortés with gifts, and the Spaniard did the same, presenting pearls and glass diamonds.

The Aztec leader guided Cortés through the streets of Tenochtitlán. He then presented a collar of colored shells to Cortés, signifying his recognition that the conquistador was Quetzalcoatl. He led Cortés to the palace of Axayacatl, located in the proximity of Moctezuma's palace. He returned and presented more gifts and after a while departed. Cortés, always a suspicious man, set up defenses, which included the strategic employment of artillery. He also decided to have brigantines built for additional protection.

The Spaniards roamed the streets of the city without any serious incident. Of particular interest was the great market. However, they also watched the human sacrifices and listened in the background to the beating drums for Huitzilopochtli. Also, the Spaniards and the Tlaxcalans were treated like royal guests; everything was provided for them, including food, women, and a drink called pulque. The entire experience only raised the suspicions of Cortés.

A moment of tension arose, however, between Cortés and Moctezuma when the two leaders climbed to the top of a pyramid. Cortés saw the bloodied walls, statues of gods, and human hearts on a brazier. The conquistador wanted to place an altar in the temple, but this time, Moctezuma stood his ground. He did agree, however, to allow the building of an altar in the palace of Axayacatl.

An event that had a meaningful impact on the relationship between Cortés and Moctezuma was the burning of Moctezuma's governor, Caulpopoca, of the province of Nautla, who was responsible, according to the Tlaxcalans, for killing the constable of Veracruz and several Spaniards in Tuxpan. The constable had led a punitive expedition for killing two conquistadors earlier; they were sent to demand allegiance to Moctezuma. Cortés became inflamed when he heard that the killings were the result of orders from Moctezuma, which the governor initially denied. Cortés became increasingly suspicious, a natural part of his personality. With the boldness that he was noted for, he kidnapped Moctezuma on November 16 in response to the killings.

Caulpopoca arrived with an entourage about three weeks later. Cortés questioned the governor, who confessed the order came from Moctezuma. Cortés demanded that Caulpopoca be burned at the stake, an action that shocked many Aztecs. If Cortés wanted to instill fear in the Aztecs, this action certainly achieved its purpose. Cortés had Moctezuma placed in chains but eventually had them removed.

One would think from this point onward the relationship between Cortés and Moctezuma would deteriorate. Ironically, just the opposite appeared to occur, at least on the surface. Cortés treated the emperor respectfully and with friendliness. They played a Mexican game; Cortés even gave Moctezuma a Spanish page. Cortés also assigned Spanish guards, and the conquistador administered discipline to any of them who mistreated the emperor. The relationship appeared so positive that Cortés even took Moctezuma hunting and boating on one of the brigantines.

Meanwhile, as the smoke and mirrors continued, dissension arose among the Aztec nobles. Cacama, the nephew of the Moctezuma and who greeted Cortés on the causeway, tried to convince the nobles to help him to kill the Spaniards. Cortés took immediate action and imprisoned the emperor's nephew and then replaced him with his brother, who eventually converted to Christianity.

Cortés now had another challenge, only this time from Cuba. His old nemesis Governor Velázquez of Cuba sent a large flotilla packed with 1,300 seasoned soldiers under the command of Panfilo de Narváez. Cortés managed to stop the force psychologically and physically. He understood what could help him gain the allegiance of the soldiers in Narváez's ranks was to tell tales of riches, which only weakened the resolve of the soldiers. Then he engaged in a battle, defeating Narváez. He then placed Narváez in chains and imprisoned him in Veracruz. While Cortés remained free and in charge, his army became unwieldy. He redistributed half of his forces, sending some of them to Veracruz and other locations.

Meanwhile, another problem surfaced. The person he left in charge while fighting Narváez, Pedro de Alvarado, took an impetuous action. During the second day of an Aztec spring festival, the captain attacked the people during the festivities. He seized leading nobles, including a military chief, hung another one, and burned at the stake the King of Nautla. He justified the attack based upon information indicating that once the festivities were over, the Aztecs would attack the Spaniards. The bloodbath only led to more bloodshed.

Upon his return, Cortés found Tenochtitlán eerily quiet, almost deserted. The bridge to the causeway was gone; the causeway itself was also damaged. Cortés sensed something was awry but not sure why, as he was unaware of Alvarado's actions. Once he arrived at the palace, he noticed that the Spaniards were under siege, which was reflected in a shortage of food and water.

Cortés then took swift, decisive action, which, being the gambler that he was, would prove costly this time. The conquistador demanded that Moctezuma order the Aztecs to resume their normal activities. Moctezuma, in a rare moment of assertiveness, said he would follow the order if Cortés released his brother, Cuitláhuac. Cortés yielded. The decision to release the emperor's brother proved disastrous because the Aztecs did not resume their daily activities nor did Cuitláhuac disappear. Moctezuma's brother convened the tlatlocan, the elective council of the Aztecs, which decided to replace Moctezuma with Cuitláhuac, who supported Cacama's revolt.

Moctezuma, protected by Spanish guards, arrived on a rooftop to speak to his people. Several chiefs recognized the Great Speaker, and they ordered the crowd to stop. Not all chiefs at the event supported Moctezuma. Aztecs below him began to shower him with arrows and stones, injuring him in multiple places; the Great Speaker died three days later. In anger, the Spaniards killed the captured nobles, along with Cacama.

Cortés then took decisive action. He decided to depart from Tenochtitlán, but it was not easy. This time, the conquistadors were on the defensive; the palace of Axayacatl had been breached. Cortés embattled his men but made another disastrous decision. He, along with his fellow warriors, would bring their gold and other precious items with them. Cortés also brought with him several women, including a mistress and two other women of great value, or so he thought: the sisters of Camaca. The group leaving with Cortés looked like a caravan; the Tlaxcalans followed along with a queue of horses and artillery. In the middle of the night, the conquistadors silently tried to work their way down a causeway but not for long. Upon reaching a canal, a woman alerted the Aztec warriors. The Aztecs bombarded the conquistadors with arrows and stones. The discipline that Cortés had engendered among the Spaniards broke. Spaniards fell into the water; some of the conquistadors lost their booty in the water and scrambled to retrieve it.

The casualties mounted. However, not just on the causeway. Cortés had divided his forces once again, leaving behind a contingent of warriors. They were defeated, humiliated, and sacrificed. Some men with Cortés faced a similar fate. In the end, Cortés lost more than 600 men but managed to escape back to Tlaxcala. Other casualties included the daughters of Moctezuma and that of Cacama. Fortunately for Cortés, some key members of his expedition survived, such as Malinche, Aguilar, Sandoval, and the volatile Alvarado.

The Spanish leader knew he had to keep his team together. He maintained his alliance with the Tlaxcalans, increased the number of soldiers in his ranks, and inculcated military discipline. He also equipped the men with guns, crossbows, and cannons. He also had prefabricated boats that would be carried to Tenochtitlán and assembled on the shore of Lake Texcoco. Cortés vowed he would return to Tenochtitlán, and the lure of gold was his reward and that of the men following him. Cortés also continued to watch his backside for potential assassination attempts because of his unstable relationship with the Velázquez faction within his ranks and the tension among his captains. He was able to manage all three, a testament to his teaming skills.

The new army and the weapons were not, however, the only killers of the Aztecs. Smallpox was a deadly weapon too. The disease spread like fire in a dry prairie, killing thousands throughout Tenochtitlán and the remainder of the empire. If that was not enough, Cortés was returning to Tenochtitlán to destroy any resistance and conquer the Aztecs.

Cortés at first reconnoitered Tenochtitlán from a distance to determine which causeways were repaired and points of weaknesses in the Aztec defenses. Then, the Spaniards along with the Tlaxacans, who carried the prefabricated boats to assemble on the shore of Lake Texcoco, crossed the waters and attacked, not without causing carnage in villages along the way prior to launching the vessels.

The Spaniards attacked from the south and west. Cortés attacked via the main causeway from the area of Xoloc, Sandoval a causeway joining at the road Acachinanco, and Alvarado the Tacuba causeway. The fighting was fierce, as the attackers faced an onslaught of rocks, arrows, barricades, body parts being hurled at them, and gaps on the causeways, and canals. Humans and horses were sacrificed at a temple in Tlatelolco. The Spaniards and Tlaxacans repeatedly were forced to retreat, facing ambushes and serious manpower losses.

A significant reason that eventually led to the Spaniards' success was the Aztec leadership fighting among themselves, even killing several of their own for not leading from the front. The Spanish and Tlaxcalan leadership were united. Cortés took advantage of the divisions among the Aztecs. Eventually, the Spaniards fought their way to the center of the city despite experiencing heavy casualties among Spaniards and Tlaxcalans, allowing the Spaniards to gain the advantage. Cuauhtémoc and other Aztecs tried to escape but were captured. After a few mop-up operations, the Spaniards had conquered Tenochtitlán.

Lessons

So, what are some key lessons (Figure 8.1) project managers can learn from the experience of Hernán Cortés on motivating?

Develop specific goals. Governor Velázquez of Cuba had issued vague goals to Hernán Cortés. He wanted the expedition to be one of discovery, not exploitation. Cortez, like many of the conquistadors, had a more specific goal: gold. This goal was something that would allow him and his fellow conquistadors to tangibly determine the success of their efforts. While it is true that this may also have been a goal of Velázquez, but that was not clearly articulated to Cortés. Velázquez, however, must have realized his mistake, or he would not have tried to stop the expedition. The corollary to this lesson is for every sponsor to carefully select a leader. Selecting the wrong person can have serious impacts on the outcome, especially if that person positions himself to challenge authority. Velázquez should have had specific goals and objectives for Cortés and his men so that everyone understood what the rewards were.

The Lessons of Hernán Cortés

- Develop specific goals
- Keep the focus on the goals
- Understand the needs of the team
- Be careful of the person chosen to run your affairs while away
- Build and maintain alliances with strategic stakeholders
- Lay the groundwork for teambuilding

Figure 8.1   The Lessons of Hernán Cortés.

Keep the focus on the goals. Cortés may not have shared the goal of the Cuban governor. Cortés, however, certainly did share his goal with his men. He knew what he and his men wanted and focused accordingly. All his actions in his expeditions were directed toward the conquest of the Aztecs as the road for acquiring gold. He had been pushed out of Tenochtitlán but was determined to return. He was willing to risk his life and those of others to achieve that goal. In the end, his accumulation of wealth garnered him not only even more wealth but power over the now destroyed empire, and he assumed many royal titles.

Understand the needs of the team. Cortés was a master of this one, and this relates to the previous lesson. He knew the motivations of the people who followed him. He knew they wanted what he wanted: gold. While the motive was base, it was nevertheless what they wanted. Even the men under Panfilo de Narváez were persuaded to follow Cortés based on the desire for gold and other precious metals. Thinking that Cortés was only using gold as a motivational tool is a mistake, though. He also knew the motivations of the natives. After engaging with the Tlaxcalans, he realized that the taste for vengeance or revenge was also a powerful motivator and used that knowledge to build a powerful alliance, which increased the odds of defeating the Aztecs.

Be careful of the person chosen to run your affairs while away. Although this lesson is applicable to Velázquez, this time it applies to Cortés and his relationship with Alvarado, who had many faults, one of which was being impetuous and having a temper. While Cortés rushed to defeat Panfilo de Narváez, Alvarado attacked an Aztec festival, which, in many ways, was the turning point of the relationship between the conquistadors and the Aztecs. Cortés had split his forces, which was a mistake, but he had not anticipated the impetuous actions of Alvarado. From that point onward, the fragile relationship between the Aztecs and the Spaniards broke, and the motivation of the Spaniards and the Tlaxcalans changed from gold to survival. Cortés realized that once he satisfied that motivation, he could return to the original motivators: gold and revenge.

Build and maintain alliances with strategic stakeholders. Effective alliances require teaming, and Cortés applied this masterfully by capitalizing on their motivations.

Even after he defeated the Tlaxcalans, he managed to build a strong relationship with them with the promise of satisfying their needs; he was able to maintain that relationship even after being pushed out of Tenochtitlán. At the same time, he was able to sustain a relationship with the Narváez faction within his force, despite it being a precarious one. Even among his officers, tension existed between Alvarado, of course, and the others, and Cortés was able to keep it under control through the promise of gold. When the conquistadors returned, Cortés prepared and, for the most part, executed a masterful three-prong attack that captured the great square of the city. The Spaniards got their gold; the Tlaxcalans got their revenge.

Lay the groundwork for teambuilding. Cortés worked at keeping the team together. He knew that he and the conquistadors had a precarious relationship with one another. Some of the conquistadors and sailors who landed with him wanted to return to Cuba with the existing gains, while another group wanted to continue. He even faced a mutiny. However, he took a bold move by destroying his fleet. The men had to ban together for no other reason than to survive in a hostile land. He recognized the need for team building, even after his escape from Tenochtitlán. He persuaded the Tlaxcalans to continue to support him and had them participate in his return to the city by carrying the prefabricated materials for the boats during the attack. He also worked with and trained the new conquistadors by imposing discipline and practicing for the eventual attack on Tenochtitlán.

Final Thoughts

Undoubtedly, Hernán Cortés was a master of motivation, albeit some people would view his techniques focused on the worse part of human nature. Nevertheless, he knew how to motivate people to support him and sustain it under truly arduous circumstances. He took advantage of the Tlaxcalans' thirst for revenge, perhaps vengeance, for against the Aztecs for seizing. He knew how to capitalize on the Spaniards' lust for gold and used that not only to conquer the Aztecs but also to defeat any forces that the governor of Cuba sent to stop him. He had figured out Moctezuma and took advantage of the emperor's weaknesses and beliefs. The ultimate masterstroke of his motivational genius was the dismantling or destruction of his ships so that no one under his command had any option but to follow him.

Successful project managers know the importance of motivating their teams. They are familiar with most of the motivational theories and know that it is an important ingredient for the success of their projects. Some project managers may not like the reliance on the base motivations used by Cortés, but the reality is that team members are motivated for many different reasons, some physiological, psychological, and sociological. Effective project managers know they need to pay particular attention to what motivates team members, individually and as a group, and how to sustain that motivation during periods when their projects appear headed toward failure and that means determining whether to use the "carrot or the stick."

Chapter 9

Jacques Cartier: Executing

Deploying a plan.

One of the most fascinating aspects of Jacques Cartier is not that he accomplished so much as an explorer but that so little is known about him. He does not seem to have the visibility of a Christopher Columbus, Ferdinand Magellan, or James Cook. Yet, his three explorations had a substantial impact, especially during his first and second expeditions, on the colonization of North America. No one knows what his appearance was; even the most famous portrait of him was created by a Russian artist prepared about three centuries later. Ironically, this human enigma set the stage for discovering one of the major rivers that would enable explorers to colonize two of the largest countries in the world: Canada and the United States.

Background

Born in 1491, just one year before Columbus discovered America, in Saint-Malo, Jacques Cartier came from a modest bourgeois family of mariners; however, he eventually married someone of much greater prominence, Catherine des Granches from a major ship-owning family. Marriage was not his only connection, either. Cartier was a relative of the abbey's treasurer, who managed to obtain visibility of the king of France, Frances I, through Bishop Le Veneur. Cartier had become a top-notch mariner with experience sailing to Brazil and Newfoundland, including possible expeditions with the navigator Giovanni da Verrazano.

What was Cartier like as a person? Little is known in this regard, too. However, some assumptions can be made based on what little is known about his past.

DOI: 10.1201/9781003028734-9

Cartier was clearly religious. Before and during his expeditions, he attended mass and planted crosses while declaring territory in the name of the king. However, this was nothing out of the ordinary since many other explorers took similar actions.

He was a brave man, as demonstrated by his trek past the shores of Newfoundland and down the St. Lawrence River, as well as his interactions with tribes like the Hurons and Iroquois.

Cartier was a resolute, determined man who sought to achieve the goals presented to him. However, he was not an idealist. He recognized the natives of North America were using him as a means to consolidate their power; he was not going to allow himself to rush into a foolhardy circumstance by returning on his third expedition to support an unreliable commander.

Naturally, leading three expeditions required considerable intelligence on Cartier's part. Bishop Le Veneur had profiled the right person to the king. Cartier's previous sailing experiences obviously provided him with solid navigational skills but also gave him the confidence to serve as a captain during all three expeditions.

Situation

The king needed someone with superb navigational skills to help make France a major maritime power equal to three other competitor nations: Spain, Portugal, and England. Spain and Portugal, of course, virtually monopolized the world of exploration, thanks largely to a papal bull issued by Pope Alexander VI, which divided the globe between the two colonizers. That changed once Pope Clement VII modified the papal bull, saying that the one by Alexander VI applied only to the global areas already discovered, not future ones. This was not surprising since Pope Clement VII's bull occurred after one of Francis I's sons married a de' Medici; now the stage was set for a man of Jacques Cartier's talents. Besides, by the time Cartier went on his first expedition, the French Bretons were already major fishermen of the Grand Banks off Newfoundland. Cartier was well prepared to take an expedition farther than other explorers, including Giovanni da Verrazano.

First Expedition

This expedition laid the groundwork for the subsequent expeditions. This one occurred in 1534. Its goals were twofold. The first one was to discover a route, known as the Northwest Passage, leading to China. The second one was to discover sources, such as islands, of gold and other precious metals. King Francis I put his full faith and credit behind the expedition. However, the king apparently caused a slight problem with the merchants of Saint-Malo, fearing that the expedition could potentially cause a manpower shortage and hurt the prosperous fishing industry.

The implementation of an embargo yielded the manpower Cartier needed to man the two vessels for the expedition, *Le Grande Hermine* and *Le Petite Hermine*. In the spring of 1534, the expedition began, taking advantage of an easterly wind and sticking to a specific latitude. The crossing of the Atlantic moved swiftly, taking a mere 20 days, leaving Saint-Malo on April 20 and reaching Cape Bonavista, Newfoundland, on May 10. From the coast of Newfoundland, apparently familiar with it due to previous expeditions under Verrazano, Cartier proceeded to discover numerous bays, capes, straits, islands, and islets without serious mishaps. Quite an achievement, having gone into unexplored areas, since he was also confronting severe fog, contrary winds, dangerous shoals, rocks, potentially hostile natives, such as the Micmac (also spelled Mi'kMaq), Huron, and Iroquois tribes. Some major places he passed or discovered included the west coast of Newfoundland, Funk Island, Quirpon Island, Sacred Island, Schooner Island, Isle au Bois, Strait of Belle Isle, Chateau Bay, Saint-Servan harbor, Islet Boulet, Steering Island, Bay of Islands, Royal, Port au Port, Magdalen Islands, Amherst Island, Prince Edward Island, Northumberland Strait, Chaleur Bay, Island Bonaventure, Gaspe Bay, and Anticosti Island.

Cartier was not too impressed with his initial discoveries, noting that many islands were full of rocks and the vegetation was of little value. However, as he progressed farther inland, he discovered that many islands were inhabited with plentiful game and vegetation, much of it consumable. On Funk Island, which he had originally named Isle of Birds, Cartier slaughtered enough gannets to fill two boats and then stored the birds in barrels. On other islands, he killed even more auks and gannets to feed the crews of both ships; he also hunted for puffins and kittiwakes, as well as spotted bears, walruses, and foxes. As for vegetation, he sighted many types of berries, including raspberries and strawberries; a wide range of trees, such as spruce, elm, and willow; and wheat, barley, and roses.

Perhaps as interesting, if not more so, was his encounters with the native tribes populating the lands that he had discovered, mainly the three already mentioned: Micmac, Huron, and Iroquois. These encounters were amiable but did not portend a positive future relationship in subsequent expeditions.

One of Cartier's first encounters was with the Micmac. Upon arrival to Chaleur Bay, a large fleet of natives approached, while Cartier and his men occupied longboats. The canoes came closer to his boat and brandished furs. Cartier knew he was outnumbered and started to return to his vessel but could not shake them. A few canoes followed, getting closer, making the Frenchmen nervous enough to fire over the natives' heads with a swivel gun while the natives danced, sang, and brandished furs. The following day, the natives returned, again displaying their furs for trade. Cartier determined that the natives were not going away. So, he turned a potentially negative situation around and sent some members of his crew ashore to trade with the natives; items traded included knives and a cape for the chief. The tactic worked with the natives, and they celebrated. Then a boat went to another location on Chaleur Bay which was greeted not only by native men but women and children too. The trading continued, but this time, the natives shared food and the French presented knives, beads, and other trinkets as gifts and some items for barter, such as for furs, even to the point that many native women accosted crew members and departed partially nude. Ever so observant, Cartier also noticed the wide variety of vegetation around the bay, including wheat, berries, and roses.

The encounters did not cease with the Micmac tribe. Cartier sent boats to explore Gaspe Bay. Once again, many canoes approached one of the boats. This encounter, however, was different because it held a person who would have a profound influence on the second and third expeditions—Chief Donnacona, from the village of Stadacona (the future site of Quebec). The relationship between the Frenchmen and the Hurons was positive, as both sides traded and exchanged gifts. The French were fascinated with the appearance of the Hurons who wore little clothing, ate their meat and fish raw, consumed maize, and had mostly shaved heads. The native women, including female children, rushed to greet Cartier and the other Frenchmen to receive tiny gifts like Hawk's bells. The entire event was a joyous exchange.

A few weeks later, the French did something that concerned the Hurons. They erected a large cross with an inscription in French, which is roughly translated as "Long Live the King" and three lilies. Right away, Donnacona recognized what the French's action meant: possession. The chief came aboard dressed in a bearskin and immediately protested and insisted that what the French did required his permission. Cartier knew he must ease the tension. Cartier then provided gifts and managed to allow the chief to relinquish his two sons, Domagaya and Taignoagny, to go to Europe with the captain and return with Cartier within a year. Much speculation of the motives exists as to why he allowed Cartier to take his two sons to Europe. One speculation is that Cartier kidnapped the boys, another is that he wanted them to bring back more goods to trade, and still another is that he feared losing his relationship with Cartier to leverage the Frenchmen against a rival, the Algonquian tribe of Maine. Whatever the reason, Cartier managed to ease the tension for the moment.

After departing from Gaspe Bay, Cartier and his fleet proceeded onward, traversing places such as Saint Peter Strait and Anticosti Island. The captain realized the weather was becoming troublesome and a longboat struck a rock. Cartier took an approach that served him well through the years. He consulted with some members of his crew and then decided it was time to return to Saint-Malo, which he did in September 1534 in just three weeks. He often consulted with members of his crew in all his expeditions; his approach was not often taken by other captains before, during, and even in later time periods.

By all accounts, the expedition was a success. He had conducted a successful exploration of the eastern part of Canada, discovered a region rich in game and vegetation, and believed that Chaleur Bay was the route leading to China. Although he had not discovered sources of gold and precious metals, he did uncover a lucrative fur trade with the natives. The gold and precious metals would come during the second expedition.

Second Expedition

This expedition, from 1535 to 1536, was perhaps the most exciting of the three expeditions. This time he would return with three vessels, *Le Grande Hermine, Le Petite Hermine*, and *L'Emerillon*, with the first one being the flagship. The primary goals of the expedition were a continuation of the first one. The first one was to continue exploration beyond Newfoundland, to include the Great River, and to seek sources of precious metals from the natives. Interestingly, finding the Northwest Passage was not a goal, perhaps because he and the king thought Chaleur Bay was the beginning of the Northwest Passage.

Cartier faced the same problems as in the first expedition when trying to find crew members for his vessels. Many seamen were indebted to the fishing merchants. The issue was surmounted once again. The vessels carried over 100 men. After attending church services, Cartier and his men were ready to disembark from Saint-Malo, doing so on May 16, 1535. This time the crossing of the Atlantic was not as smooth as the first expedition despite following closely the previous route. Facing the tumultuous ocean swells and fierce contrary winds, the vessels lost one another; *Le Grande Hermine* stopped at Funk Island and once again killed and salted boatloads of auks; the vessel then proceeded to Blanc Sablon where the other two vessels made rendezvous, refilling water casks and making necessary repairs. The vessels then sailed to the Strait of Belle Isle, other islands, and continued westward, planting a large wooden cross along the way to aid in directing the other two vessels. Domagaya and Taignoagny guided Cartier to Saguenay at the Hochelaga River. He continued onward along the coast, passing many islands until he reached Saguenay, passing cliffs and steep banks, sailing through rapids, and passing through shoals. All three vessels masterly made it through and stopped at a place called Todousacc where they encountered Huron fishing but only briefly. The vessels continued, but not without *L'Emerillon* barely managing to escape grounding. Once the flood tide arrived, the vessels again passed by a dozen islands, some that had plenty of edible vegetation and game. Cartier set anchor and once again encountered a Huron fishing party, which this time provided food, such as maize, eel, and fish, for the French crews. Chief Donnacona, the father of Domagaya and Taignoagny, came aboard *Le Grande Hermine* with warriors. The meeting with his sons and Cartier was positive.

Cartier explored upstream, arriving at the point where the Great River and the St. Charles River converged. At the shore was Stadacona (close to where Quebec is located today). Cartier and some crew members came ashore on boats. The natives greeted them singing and dancing; Cartier distributed gifts and then returned to his vessels. Both *Le Grande Hermine* and *Le Petite Hermine* were guided to the fork by Donnacona and his canoes. This time Donnacona and his two sons came aboard. The discussion turned to business. Donnacona attempted to dissuade Cartier from going to Hochelaga (near contemporary Montreal) for fear of losing the French captain as an ally; the chief in Hochelaga sought dominion over Donnacona. Determined to keep Cartier, Donnacona made offers of his niece and young boys as an expression of affection, which Cartier rejected, and then tried one other tactic. He brought on board medicine men in an attempt to scare Cartier from going to Hochelaga; Cartier remain unphased and decided to proceed without the help of one of the chief's sons guiding the vessels to Hochelaga. Donnacona settled with a couple of washbasins and a 12-gun salute.

The *L'Emerillon* towed two longboats as it proceeded masterfully toward Hochelaga despite turbulent waters. At one point, they encountered a group of natives camped on the shore known as Achelacy (later known as Notre Dame de Pontneuf), exchanged gifts with them, and continued through the rapids, passing St. Maurice until they reached a spot in the Great River with five channels. Again, Cartier encountered natives who were hunting and directed him through the one leading to Hochelaga. After mooring *L'Emerillon*, Cartier and some crew members took longboats and traded along the way. Their reception was nothing like what they experienced when they reached Hochelaga. Over a thousand Hurons greeted them with food and gifts. A long night of celebration ensued as the natives danced and howled at Cartier and his men as they entered a heavily protected town. He entered a spacious dwelling replete with corn and game and a large fire. A paralyzed chief hoisted upon a deerskin carrier supported by several natives confronted them. The chief was known as the "Chief Lord of the Country," and he wanted Cartier to touch him and, having done so, read a passage from the Bible. Cartier offered gifts and sounded trumpets, which only excited the natives even more. Soon thereafter, Cartier climbed Mont Royal, and he recognized the rapids, called the Lachine Rapids, which appeared almost impossible to pass through. Beyond those rapids was another river called the Ottawa leading to the Kingdom of the Saguenay which was protected by fierce warriors and was full of precious metals, such as gold and silver. Cartier and his men, some by piggyback, returned to *L'Emerillon*. Cartier sailed the *L'Emerillon* down St. Maurice to meet with *Le Grande Hermine* and *L'Petite Hermine*. Once again, Cartier met with Donnacona and exchanged gifts. This time Donnacona had a special presentation for Cartier: scalps. It was an effort to impress Cartier with the warrior fierceness of his people.

Cartier and his crew spent the winter of 1535–1536 near what is known as Quebec as his vessels were frozen in place within an ice sheet. The men built a small fort and provisioned it with game, fish, and vegetation. Two key events occurred while the French men hunkered for the winter. Cartier prepared his journal. The crew also came down with scurvy, but they managed to save most of them with an elixir made from the boiled bark of a spruce tree provided by none other than Domagaya. Donnacona had amplified the wealth of the Kingdom of Saguenay so much so that Cartier kidnapped the chief, Domagaya, Taignoagny, and several other natives and took them back to France. The goal was to have Donnacona tell the French king about what he had told Cartier. The captain promised to return them within a year with gifts. As a quid pro quo for the moment, Cartier left the *Le Petite Hermine* for the natives to ransack, especially the iron from the hull. The other two vessels returned in July 1536 at Saint-Malo after losing approximately 25 percent of the crew.

Third Expedition

This expedition was far from anticlimactic but lacked any notable achievement. The goals were twofold: find the Kingdom of Saguenay (and the gold residing there) and establish a permanent colony. The expedition from the perspective of achieving those goals was a dismal failure. However, the cause was not Cartier but his commander of the expedition, Jean-François de La Rocque, sieur Roberval, or Roberval for short.

Francis I was excited about the Kingdom of Saguenay and rewarded Cartier with ownership of the *Le Grande Hermine*, which he was purported to use to raid Spanish and Portuguese vessels; he also rewarded Cartier financially and appointed him captain-general. Cartier prepared for the third expedition, identifying all the resources required to complete an expedition, including establishing a settlement. Some of the manpower for the settlement included convicts.

The king put in overall charge for the expedition his friend, Roberval, now the lieutenant-general; Robervali negatively impacted the execution of the expedition. He had broad powers over the expedition and throughout French Canada but felt he lacked just about everything, especially money, provisions, and artillery. He ended up staying behind, seeking the patronage of an Italian merchant and pirating vessels in the English Channel, supposedly to raise the resources he needed to go to Canada. In the interim, Roberval had sent Cartier ahead.

The expedition crossed the Atlantic started in April 1541 with five vessels. Like the previous expedition, the crossing was difficult due to inclement weather, taking almost a full month and causing three vessels to separate from the fleet, resulting in the loss of boats. Cartier did manage to trade with the natives on the western side of Newfoundland.

Cartier's luck seemed to reverse itself. In August 1541, he made it to Stadacona, and he met with the new chief known as Agona. He and his crew members were positively received and subsequently sailed in boats up to Cape Rouge; all five of his vessels followed. Almost right away, the colonists established the settlement; Cartier sent two of the vessels back. The settlement, known as Charlesbourg-Royal, was also to serve as a base to discover the Kingdom of Saguenay. Naturally, the Hurons saw the settlement as a takeover and became hostile. Fearless, Cartier continued to pursue the Kingdom of Saguenay by returning, in boats, to the Lord of Hochelaga; the lord received the Frenchman on friendly terms and provided guides to take him to the kingdom. He encountered another group of friendly natives at a village; here he learned about a serious sault. Cartier decided to return to the settlement but first stopped at Achelacy to meet with the chief, only to discover later he was with Agona in Hochelaga. Cartier's brother-in-law indicated that the natives were acting suspiciously and soon thereafter they attacked the settlement. Cartier decided to depart with the colonists after having lost 35 of them. Of course, they departed with the precious metals and diamonds that they had acquired.

And where was Roberval? Off the coast of Newfoundland, almost one year later. Cartier refused to return to the settlement with Roberval, claiming it was impossible to defend the settlement; Cartier had refused the orders of the lieutenant-general. Cartier returned to Saint-Malo in October 1542 with a load of gold and diamonds, only to find out that the contents were iron pyrite (commonly known as fool's gold) and quartz.

Lessons

So, what are some of the key lessons (Figure 9.1) project managers can learn from the experience of Jacques Cartier about executing?

Expect resistance during execution from some stakeholders. Cartier faced resistance right from the start. He faced resistance from the merchants of Saint-Malo because they feared he would drain manpower from their commercial fishing ventures. However, he also received resistance from somewhere else that only a powerful person like Francis I could provide. Charles V of Spain also opposed the expedition. Charles V put his spies to work and even solicited the power of the church to dissuade Francis I from allowing the expeditions. But to no avail. Charles V riddled Paris, Saint-Malo, and other ports to collect as much information about the expedition as possible. Another important party, of course, included the Hurons, who originally were supportive of the French but eventually turned due to some of

The Lessons of Jacques Cartier

- Expect resistance from some stakeholders during execution
- Leverage prior experience
- Be flexible and adaptable when encountering the unexpected
- Establish and main relationships with stakeholders who can impact the chance of success
- Make honest assessments of circumstances
- Be willing to "push the envelope"
- Be willing to say "no"
- Consult with the right people

Figure 9.1 The Lessons of Jacque Cartier.

Cartier's actions, such as kidnapping Donnacona and erecting a cross while simultaneously declaring the area a territory of France.

Leverage prior experience. The first expedition for Cartier provided him with useful information for his subsequent ones. He followed quite closely with the same route as the first one and knew what resources, such as auks, salmon, and maize, to exploit during the second and third ones. He also leveraged his contacts with two native tribes, the Micmacs and Hurons, made from the first expedition. He learned about the Great River, other natives downriver, and the Kingdom of Saguenay.

Be flexible and adaptable when encountering the unexpected. Cartier knew how to be flexible and adaptable during his expeditions. He realized that he needed to use longboats rather than the larger ships, such as the *Le Grande Hermine*, when entering shoals and rapids. He also did not overreact when canoes filled with natives approached his ships or longboats.

Establish and maintain positive relationships with stakeholders who can impact the chance of success. When encountering the Hurons, he was willing to work with, not change, their customs. He also used the encounters to lessen tension by offering gifts, such as cloaks to chiefs and hawks' bells to children, as well as having crew members participate in their dancing and singing. In other words, he made a concerted effort to develop a positive relationship with the natives up to a certain point. The relationships changed when he claimed the territory for France and kidnapped Donnacona. Such arrogant actions inevitably impacted the relationships and reached a breaking point during the third expedition with the colonists settling in the area.

Make honest assessments of circumstances. Cartier was rooted in realism, not idealism. He may have wanted to convert the natives to Christianity, but that was not his primary motive. Francis I played the Christian card over fear that the papacy would change its mind about allowing France to become a major colonial power on the level of a Portugal or Spain. In the end, conversion was not realistic despite reading passages from the gospel to the ailing chief of Hochelaga, planting crosses during territorial seizure of land for France, and converting Donnacona to Christianity. Cartier was also honest in his assessments about the territories and the customs of the natives when preparing his journals. For example, the initial explorations of the first expedition appeared unimpressive to him, and he recorded his impressions. He also understood native customs and behaviors despite some moral prejudices of the time that affected his assessments, such as the nakedness of the native women.

Be willing to "push the envelope." Cartier was a risk-taker but not a foolish one. On his first expedition, he was dissatisfied with the results. He still wanted to continue west of Newfoundland. He discovered many bays, islands, rivers, capes, and, most importantly, the Great River and Chaleur Bay, as well as the villages of Stadacona and Hochelaga, future sites of Quebec and Montreal, respectively. His willingness to proceed forward to acquire more information to accomplish the goals of his expeditions led to encountering tribes like the Micmacs, Hurons, and Iroquois, despite the warnings from Donnacona about going to Hochelaga. Cartier did not, however, take foolish chances. When he approached the Lechine Rapids during the third expedition in search of the Kingdom of Saguenay, he recognized the futility of proceeding and decided to return to Charlesbourg-Royal. Upon his return, the attack by the Hurons occurred, and he realized he lacked the manpower to remain.

Be willing to say "no." In addition to deciding against proceeding toward the legendary Kingdom of Saguenay, Cartier knew when "no" was the right answer, just like with the rapids. Upon returning to Saint-Malo on the third expedition, he and Roberval finally gathered after the latter being almost one year late. Roberval ordered Cartier to return to Charlesbourg-Royal, but Cartier knew that would be foolish, even disastrous, and refused to follow the order. He headed back to France. History proved him right; Roberval was forced to return to France, thanks to wars with the natives and diseases.

Consult with the right people. During his expeditions, Cartier was wise enough to consult with crew members when situations required it. He knew the decision would ultimately be his own; however, he recognized the value of soliciting advice, which was rare among the early explorers. An example was when he had to determine when to return to Saint-Malo on his first expedition.

Final Thoughts

Jacques Cartier knew how to execute an expedition. He knew the vision and goal, focused on both, received the backing of key sponsors like the king and the papacy, and required the necessary resources to have a successful execution. When an unexpected event arose, he sent advance parties to collect more information and data to deal effectively with it, whether it involved natives or terrain. When he had trouble deciding what to do under certain situations, he did not hesitate to consult with members of his crew. He knew how to work with the natives he encountered and, for the most part, maintained a positive relationship until the third expedition when the interaction with the natives and Roberval became strained and eventually broke down. Even then, he recognized the reality of the situation related to the colony and decided to return to France over the objections of Roberval.

Effective project managers know that their experience is a great teacher, albeit sometimes painful. They know how to leverage that knowledge on future projects. Most of all, they have the courage to be honest with themselves and others. They are also willing to take the dangerous action of saying "no" to an impractical project despite the consequences. They have no problem asking the right people for information, data, and advice about activities and situations. They also know how to get data, information, and advice by developing and sustaining a positive relationship with stakeholders.

Chapter 10

Vasco da Gama: Embracing the Unknown

Recognizing that sometimes having the courage to pursue a goal requires facing indeterminable risks.

Vasco da Gama, born circa 1460, entered the ranks of history as an accomplished captain-major of a small fleet of four vessels. The Portuguese fleet performed a trans-ocean, transcontinental expedition that increased trade, such as spices, between Europe and Asia. He also weakened the stranglehold over that trade monopolized by Italian merchants, such as ones from Genoa, and the Muslims. While it did not eliminate that trade by way of the Italians and the Muslims, it had a debilitating effect on their stranglehold.

This expedition was truly one that entered the unknown once da Gama's vessels boomeranged across the Atlantic Ocean and rounded the Cape of Good Hope. Keep in mind, too, that da Gama's expedition was just a few years after Columbus took his own exploration to the Western Hemisphere. The Portuguese, of course, already had a good knowledge of the west coast of Africa, thanks largely to other explorers. When da Gama circled the Cape of Good Hope, all previous experiences in terms of what to expect seemed no longer relevant.

Background

Vasco da Gama came from a prominent, politically connected, military family whom King Manuel could trust. Da Gama's father, Estêvão, had served as a knight for the Duke of Viseu, a member of the prestigious Military Order of Christ, and

DOI: 10.1201/9781003028734-10

a civil governor for Viseu. His mother, Isabel Sodre, was well-connected, too, and was of English descent and had connections with the Duke of Viseu. Da Gama, despite his noble background, proved his military prowess just as his father had done. Vasco da Gama served the king fighting pirates and the French off the coast of Portugal. Under such conditions, he learned the art of command and navigation.

Despite his background, da Gama was not a perfect man. He had his foibles. He was known to be temperamental, an extreme disciplinarian, rigid, formal, bold, resolute, and cruel. In his eyes, King Manuel had picked the right man.

Situation

King Manuel I, who succeeded King João III, was facing domestic concerns, the dominance of other countries like Spain, and the throttling of the spice trade by the Muslims and Italians. The king needed to turn to someone who had military and command experience and was of noble birth. The name of Vasco da Gama came to mind.

Expedition

However, traveling into the unknown required additional talent and experience. Da Gama had the benefit of a team of experienced officers, one of which was Bartolomeu Dias, the famed Portuguese explorer who was the first to reach the Cape of Good Hope; Dias had accompanied da Gama's expedition to the Cape Verde Islands. Da Gama had three additional officers of considerable knowledge and experience: Pero Alemquer, Gonçalo Nunes, and Nicolau Coelho.

Da Gama knew he was going into the unknown; however, he was prepared. He had four small but well-built vessels under his command to take him to his destination, Calicut. These vessels were the *São Gabriel*, *São Rafael*, *Berrio*, and an unknown storage boat. What made the *São Gabriel* and *São Rafael* special was that they were built under the supervision of Dias. The *Berrio* was a lighter vessel than the others to enable quick reconnaissance along the African coast. The storage boat was no less important because it carried three years of provisions, to include salted meats, vegetables, water, and seasonings; it also carried ample supplies of token gifts to distribute along the way to and at Calicut; the quality of the gifts posed a significant challenge with certain relationships along the way. Just as importantly, all the other vessels carried extra rigging, spars, ropes, and sails, which would help keep the vessels in operating order, or so he thought. He also had crews with several skills, ranging from carpenters and musicians to gunners and interpreters.

Da Gama was now ready to achieve three goals that King Manual had assigned to him. The first one was to discover additional lands of value to Portugal. In other words, add to the colonial real estate of the Portuguese Empire, only this time not just in Africa but also in Asia. The second one was to spread Christianity to the peoples of these areas and to contact other Christian kingdoms, including ones of the legendary Prester John. The third and final one was to build trade relationships in the spice and precious stones trade that enhanced Portugal's wealth and power.

In July 1497, after attending a church service and receiving Holy Communion at Rostelo, da Gama was ready to head to the Cape Verde Islands, like so many other Portuguese explorers of the past; the expedition required traveling 1,600 miles to the islands with his crew of 170 men, which included some men of questionable character. Stopping at the Cape Verde Islands, located off the coast of Senegal, enabled his fleet to replenish provisions and perform maintenance on the vessels. At the Cape Verde Islands, Bartolomeu Dias left the fleet.

Now da Gama was ready to display the boldness and determination that added to his fame. Instead of following along the coast of West Africa to the Cape of Good Hope, he decided to take his fleet far into the mid-Atlantic to avoid contrary winds and capture winds and currents to "jettison" his fleet around the Cape of Good Hope. (Interestingly, he had almost made it to Brazil.) This route had never been chosen before and was a remarkable achievement despite having a negative impact on the crew. He took his fleet truly into the unknown without sea charts, no previous experience among his officers, and no way to determine longitude. The route was long, thanks to the doldrums, and was heading south until he caught the easterlies and a current. The entire ordeal took 80 days and approximately 4,000 miles; ran provisions low, such as water; and required repairs to vessels. After all that, the fleet did not end up passing the Cape of Good Hope. Instead, he had to proceed partially down the west coast of Africa, coming to a bay that he named St. Helena, which ended in a hostile experience with the natives throwing spears; it all seemed to serve as a forewarning of the troubles to come.

Circling around the Cape of Good Hope, da Gama came upon a coastline that he named Natal and then engaged with natives on a river that he had named the River of Good Tokens; the relationship with the natives was an improvement over the one they had with the natives they had met at the Bay of St. Helena. However, the natives communicated the same issue that da Gama was to hear just about all the way to Calicut: they were unimpressed with the gifts and trade goods that they offered. Da Gama was going to face a world completely different from the one he had known on the west coast of Africa.

Continuing northward along the east coast of Africa, they arrived at Mozambique, encountering Muslims and Arab vessels, the latter carrying precious metals, jewels, and spices. Many of the people were dressed in fine silken clothing laced with gold. The local sultan came aboard the *São Gabriel* and expressed his displeasure with the Portuguese and that he was unimpressed with the gifts and goods they had to offer. Bracelets, bells, and beads were just not that impressive, as they would have been on the west coast of Africa, although some trading did occur.

Da Gama departed farther north but the current made it difficult to proceed, and the expedition had to return to Mozambique to obtain provisions. The reception turned decidedly negative. His fleet was accosted by a hostile group of Mozambicans, which resulted in da Gama firing his cannons; the situation then settled tenuously until the fleet continued north.

The fleet arrived in Mombasa, and the Portuguese would not fare any better in terms of relationships with the local populace. Several dhows approached, flags waving, and gave the Portuguese the impression that locals, about 100 of them, were coming to visit them were Christians were living among the Moors; actually, the locals were celebrating the end of Ramadan. Da Gama became suspicious of their motives; however, nothing happened.

The sultan then presented gifts of fruit and sheep and two "Christians" for protection if someone came ashore. Da Gama then sent two crew members to meet the sultan and encountered Christian merchants and images of the Holy Ghost when, in fact, they were Hindi; the men returned. Being suspicious, da Gama kidnapped two locals and tortured them for information. Then one evening, the crew heard the cutting of cables as the Hindi tried unsuccessfully to board the vessels. Da Gama had captured close to 20 of them; the captain-major did not release them until his next stop on the east coast of Africa, Malindi.

Malindi was a different experience for da Gama for one simple reason. The sultan needed an ally against his counterpart in Mombasa and, therefore, was very accommodating to the needs of da Gama. The Portuguese vessels appeared powerful with their cannons, and, if needed, they would be devastating against the sultan of Mombasa.

The captain-major encountered Indian vessels and invited some of the Indian crew aboard *São Rafael*. The Indians saw a figure of the Virgin Mary and came to their knees, thinking it was a Hindi god, and da Gama thought they had come across Christians.

Da Gama met with the sultan, and the experience was positive for the reason previously mentioned. The sultan was in lavish surroundings in a vessel coming to greet da Gama. The men exchanged gifts; the sultan gave the Portuguese spices and sheep. But he gave da Gama something even more important. The sultan also offered a pilot to guide da Gama to Calicut. This guide would not have to be tortured and punished like the ones da Gama had captured earlier and who proved of little value.

The pilot truly was a valuable gift to da Gama. He guided the captain-major and his vessels through treacherous waters replete with many islands and atolls, which threatened to lose and destroy his remaining three vessels. Da Gama also had the power of a monsoon behind him, enabling his fleet to reach the Malabar coast of India in just 23 days.

Da Gama and his fleet were initially greeted with a celebration on the part of the zamorin, or ruler, of Calicut. An emissary of the ruler came aboard to invite the Portuguese captain-major to the palace. Da Gama was carried on a palanquin supported by six men and along came 13 of his men. Leading the way was a queue of sword carrying and trumpet blasting Indians. The Portuguese entered a temple, which they misconstrued as a Christian church. They encountered a sight unseen before by a Portuguese sailor: a man sitting on a couch, chewing betel nuts, and spitting into a golden bowl. The ruler called for fruits to be delivered for his new visitors. Not only did he misconstrue the Indians as Christians, but da Gama also offered an array of gifts that the ruler and his direct minions construed as an insult. The zamorin expected something of greater value, specifically the golden statue of the Virgin Mary, which da Gama declined to offer as a gift. Instead, da Gama promised a lucrative trade between Portugal and Calicut, exchanging precious metals and purple cloth for spices and precious stones. Tension mounted as da Gama's suspicious personality overcame him; a palanquin carried him back to his ship as the rest of his entourage returned later.

For a while, da Gama was permitted to trade cargo for supplies. However, that only added to the suspicions and tensions because most of the traders were Arabs who did not care for the Christian Portuguese, to the point of not even engaging in trade. Suffice it to say, the trading was not very lucrative for the Portuguese.

Still, da Gama left two of his men, one of which was Diogo Dias (the brother of Bartolomeu Dias), with the zamorin in exchange for taking back to Portugal Indians from the ruler's court. The situation deteriorated when the zamorin wanted da Gama to pay duties. Da Gama became even more suspicious, even concluding that his men were being held captive. Da Gama then seized hostages, but they were soon released when the captain-general was convinced that the men were not being held against their will.

Da Gama decided to return to Portugal after a short trip just south of Goa, India, stopping for provisions and repairs. The return trip was brutal, having no pilot, and sailing across the Indian Ocean navigating through the many islands, such as the Laccadive Islands, and the countless atolls. They also faced monsoon winds and scurvy, killing so many of his crew that he lacked sufficient men to man the *São Rafael* and destroyed it off the coast of Africa. The return to Portugal could have been even more disastrous if he had not stopped off the coast of Malindi; the sultan provided provisions and a gift for King Manuel.

Left with a fraction of the crew they started with and half the vessels, the fleet headed toward Cape Verde Islands. The *Berrio* continued to Portugal, while the *São Gabriel* had one more task to complete, this time in the Azores. Da Gama faced a tragedy with his brother, Paolo, who died and was buried on the islands. The *São Gabriel* returned to Lisbon in September 1499, where da Gama received a grand welcome, a gold coin issued in his honor, and eventually the title of viceroy.

Lessons

So, what are some of the key lessons (Figure 10.1) project managers can learn from Vasco da Gama's experience of embracing the unknown?

The Lessons of Vasco da Gama

- Avoid assuming and treating all stakeholders the same
- Avoid allowing paradigms and prejudices to dominate thinking
- Rely on local talent
- Recognize experience is important
- Prepare for the known unknowns
- Be ready to face the setbacks and do whatever is required to overcome them

Figure 10.1   The Lessons of Vasco da Gama.

Avoid assuming and treating all stakeholders the same. Da Gama continued throughout his voyage with this perspective about his stakeholders. He treated just about all of his encounters with other civilizations the same, thinking they were alike when, in fact, they were not. Not only were the customs different but so was what they considered valuable. Bells, butter, honey, hats, and the like may have worked with some parties on the west coast of Africa but not on the other side of the continent and in India. Except in Malindi, the results were the same. Much of his perception was based on what was known about other people at the time on the west coast of Africa, and he relied on that knowledge. But it proved a costly perception.

Avoid allowing paradigms and prejudices to dominate thinking. Da Gama was a product of his times, just as everyone is. These paradigms and their accompanying prejudices that predominate in a culture affect how people perceive their world and how they respond or react to it. Da Gama let the paradigms and prejudices of his time control him. He often fell into the trap of viewing Hindus as Christians simply by being eclectic in how he viewed and interpreted their behavior, resulting in conflict with other peoples in east Africa and India.

Rely on local talent. Da Gama recognized that to accomplish his goal of reaching Calicut, he needed to seek help from people who knew the cultural and physical terrain. He was willing to accept the offer from a sultan to provide a pilot to help him reach the city. The pilot proved invaluable, and his absence contributed to the crews' difficult return to the east coast of Africa. Of course, having pilots by kidnapping them as da Gama had done earlier in Mombasa did not prove fruitful.

Recognize experience is important. Da Gama recognized that experience counts when entering the unknown. He had navigational knowledge, but that was not one of his strengths. He needed people with experience and received it. Bartolomeu Dias supervised the building of the two main vessels of his fleet, *São Gabriel* and *São Rafael*. Da Gama relied upon him up to but not beyond the Cape Verde Islands. Still, he had Bartolomeu's brother, Diogo, who was an experienced sailor, along with Nicolau Coehlo of the *Berrio*. Armed with such experience, he was able to traverse deep into the Atlantic Ocean and pass around the Cape of Good Hope. He was also willing to use local experience to help him reach his destination.

Prepare for the known unknowns. Da Gama had a shortfall in this regard. He did provide provisions for a three-year journey, which not only included food but also ropes, spars, etc. Unfortunately, he experienced some setbacks, which perhaps he should have considered. He did not anticipate losing two vessels, the storeship and *São Rafael*, albeit he was able to develop workarounds by redistributing provisions, supplies, and crew members. He did not expect that he would encounter natives on the east coast of Africa who were dramatically different from the ones on the west coast, or he would have brought better gifts. He also did not anticipate that some native populations would be hostile, although three of his vessels were armed with cannons. He seemed to conduct the expedition from the perspective of what he knew, not anticipating problems that lay ahead.

Be ready to face the setbacks and do whatever is required to overcome them. Da Gama was determined to reach Calicut, connect with other Christians (even though they were Hindi), and identify sources of gold, precious gems, and spices. Nothing was going to impede his goals. He was willing to destroy two of his four vessels if it meant proceeding to Calicut and returning to Portugal. He was willing to not waste time in ports that impeded his progress, such as in Mombasa, even if it meant employing kidnapping. He was determined to return to Lisbon, even at the expense of losing many of his crew to scurvy.

Final Thoughts

Vasco da Gama experienced the trials and tribulations of leading an expedition into the unknown world of exploration. He had tackled what he knew of previous explorations, but he also was willing to pursue routes never traversed, at least by the Portuguese. He took a wide loop into the Atlantic Ocean so that he could pass by the Cape of Good Hope, which he eventually did but not without hardship upon his crew. He entered ports on the east coast of Africa only to have two negative encounters and even one at his destination. If he had any major flaw, it was his false assumption that everyone on the east coast of Africa and Calicut was the same in terms of needs and expectations as the people on the west side of that continent. Most of the people of the east coast of Africa were not of the same religion nor did they have an interest in, for example, glass beads.

Project managers, whether realizing it or not, embrace the unknown. Not everything can be defined in a plan. Some risks and issues can be anticipated, but not everyone can do that. To move a project into the unknown with minimal definition upfront can be exhilarating and exasperating at the same time. Through a combination of applying good project and risk management disciplines, they can minimize the impact of the unknown and not have to deal with risks and issues as they arise as Vasco da Gama did. While da Gama was not totally ignorant of the risk and issues facing him, such as they relate to supplies and equipment, he appeared to have overlooked the needs and wants of stakeholders along the way. Effective project managers know they must consider the risks and issues impacting all aspects of their projects, such as people, processes, systems, and data.

Chapter 11

Vitus Bering: Staying on Track

Following a plan to achieve a goal or end-state despite incentives or other inducements to go astray.

That Vitus Bering was an explorer par excellence is without question. He led two expeditions that made major discoveries for Russia. Unfortunately, Bering is more of an example of how not to remain on track than how to stay on track. Still, his experience provides useful lessons on what to do and avoid when executing a plan to achieve a goal.

Background

Bering had a unique background. Few people realize that he was not Russian; he was a Dane who served initially in the court of Peter the Great who wanted to bring his country's naval forces up to the same standard as the European powers. Like other great explorers, Bering found that being a foreigner in charge of an expedition consisting primarily of another population had its challenges. He was a Lutheran in charge of a team that was not only primarily Russian but also of a different religion, Russian Orthodox. His competency and experience gave him the means to overcome the challenge and enabled him to move rapidly up the hierarchy of the Russian navy.

He was born the son of Jonas Svendsen and Anne Pedersdatter, the former being a customs inspector and a churchwarden. His brother, a bit of a rowdy lad, participated in a riot, which resulted in him being exiled as a customer collector in India; Bering tagged along with his brother. Bering seized the opportunity

DOI: 10.1201/9781003028734-11

to learn about sailing, from working on vessels to navigating the high seas as he worked for Dutch and Danish captains. He then trained to become a naval officer in Amsterdam. Eventually, he joined the Russian Imperial Navy and participated in the Great Northern War, performing so well that he rapidly rose through the ranks despite not experiencing any naval battles. His marriage to Anna Christina Pulse, who came from a wealthy Swedish family, and his connections with Admiral Cornelius Cruys, a close trusted friend of Peter the Great, probably helped his career. Regardless, Bering was recognized as a man of great talent who exhibited many qualities of leadership, such as bravery, resoluteness, decisiveness, and patience, and he could be counted on to follow orders.

Situation

Peter the Great was striving to make Russia a significant power equivalent to those of western Europe. One aspiration was to have a significant discovery of other lands, in this case America. To add fuel to the fire, the English, Dutch, and French were enlarging their presence in the northern part of the Pacific Ocean. Peter the Great decided to sponsor an expedition under the command of Bering which, subsequently, resulted in a second expedition.

First Expedition

This expedition laid the groundwork for the second one. It primarily focused on identifying the geographical extent of the Asian continent and determining whether the Asian and North American continents joined north of the Kamchatka Peninsula. Bering was also responsible for mapping the journey to Kamchatka and from there to the Arctic Ocean.

Right from the start, the expedition experienced delays. Part of the problem was procuring the resources necessary to execute the expedition. On one hand, the expedition was ladened with supplies to build boats, barges, bridges, and living quarters, but this only contributed to delaying the expedition and even a shortfall occurred with these items. On the other hand, the expedition was short of other essential supplies, equipment, and manpower, which required sending advance parties to collect more of the same at such places as Yakutsk and Irkutsk. The trouble with Yakutsk and Irkutsk, for example, was that the cooperation did not exist or was inadequate because Bering faced corrupt, uncooperative governors. Some settlements did not have enough manpower or were reluctant to provide any men. Many men became sick or deserted, and horses died for lack of grass.

Other challenges presented difficulties during his 6,000-mile journey to Kamchatka. His men crossed through frigid, windy mountain passes, frozen rivers covered with thin, long blizzards, and trekked through bog and inadequate roads, while at the same time suffering from hunger, tiredness, and weakness, which resulted in many of them becoming hostile. Even after reaching Kamchatka, neither the natives nor the Siberians were cooperative, rebelling in some instances.

Despite the delays, insurrections, desertions, disease, and scraping for provisions, the expedition was able to continue Bering and his officers, which included Martin Spanberg and Aleksei Chirikoff, prepared the vessel the *Archangel Gabriel* to serve as the primary vessel for the expedition departing Kamchatka. The goal of the first expedition, which was vague, as opposed to the second expedition, was to sail northward along the shore. In early July, the *Archangel Gabriel* embarked on the first expedition.

The journey was unpleasant. The men subsisted on a limited diet of fish oil, sea biscuits, dried fish, a fermented drink, and water. The crew became disgruntled. During the journey, however, the *Archangel Gabriel* discovered the St. Lawrence Island and the Diomede Islands. The real challenge came when the *Archangel Gabriel* came close to discovering America; the fog and stormy weather made it difficult for a landing in America and so Bering dispensed with sheltering for the winter and returned to Kamchatka in early September. This decision would soon tarnish Bering's reputation; he would be accused of lacking the necessary bravery to wait out the winter and to continue the exploration during the upcoming spring or summer. While he failed to land in America, he was convinced that the two continents did not meet, despite the weather impeding his visibility. He also managed to map the Siberian coastline and its territories, and he discovered islands, specifically St. Lawrence and Diomede Islands.

Second Expedition

Bering, a commander with resolve and under attack by members of the Russian Senate, pushed for a second expedition, leaving from Kamchatka. Known as the Great Expedition, this one was an expansion of the first one. Not only did the scope expand but also the challenges, which ended in the death of Vitus Bering.

The primary goals were to discover America by sailing from Kamchatka, confirm whether a bridge existed between Asia and America, and map the coastline of Siberia. Other goals included reaching Japan from Siberia and setting up a postal system through eastern Russia.

As with the first expedition, Bering hauled a massive quantity of supplies and equipment just to return to Kamchatka and build two vessels, eventually named *St. Peter* and *St. Paul*. Like the previous expedition, he sent advance parties on the way to Tobolsk and Yakutsk, in 1733, to obtain more provisions, but he received pushback and a lack of cooperation. Spanberg, an officer on Bering's first expedition, also experienced trouble from a major general at Okhotsk; the general was exiled in Siberia over political and corruption charges.

The journey across was just as challenging, if not more so, on the way to Kamchatka. Bering and his advanced parties dealt with the severe weather. His and his officers' "wagon train" faced natural obstacles crossing rivers, which resulted in losing barges and boats. Also, his own officers and the professors who had joined the expedition contributed to the challenges. Many of the professors expected special treatment and housing appropriate to their status and complained constantly. His officers wanted their families to accompany them, which added to the burden, requiring even more provisions and housing. To increase Bering's troubles, the mother of his nephew also complained to the court about her son's treatment. Then, Georg Steller, a scientist, elevated his complaints about Bering to the leaders within his church and the Russian Senate. The court sent a sergeant to collect feedback about the overall performance of the expedition from the perspective of the subordinates; fortunately, the officers complained that their time was limited, and they had no opportunity to prepare a report. Many crew members were drunks and former criminals, which only added to Bering's woes. Since natives were forced to assist, from food to manpower, they rebelled, devasting villages and even killing soldiers; retaliation came with the massacre of villagers at Utkolotsk.

Despite all these challenges and the expedition falling further behind schedule, the two vessels, *St. Peter* and *St. Paul*, were ready to start their journey in 1741. The vessels required a large quantity of provisions, such as dried pork, beef, fish, salt, flour, and, perhaps the most critical of all supplies, water. During the entire expedition, the pursuit of potable water across the Pacific Ocean was a major contributing factor in determining priorities. The quantity of water was underestimated, partly because Bering had expected the trip to America would only take a week. In addition to provisions, the crew was substantially larger than during the first expedition. Both the *St. Peter* and *St. Paul* also had an impressive crew in terms of skills. A substantial number of marines and sailors with the *St. Peter* were supported with cannons, cannonballs, and gunpowder. Bering himself had a supporting staff, consisting of four senior officers (who made up the sea council), and a physician, musician, and servants. Underneath, the command structure consisted of junior officers with a range of responsibilities from ensuring the deck and maintaining order throughout the ship. Other crew members included carpenters, blacksmiths, and interpreters.

One of the major responsibilities, as with other great expeditions, was updating the ship's log with critical information daily. This information included speed, wind direction, observations, knots, repairs, landings, longitude, and latitude. To ensure accuracy, two officers separately completed a log.

Another major responsibility was convening the sea council. An interesting approach in the Russian navy was that it required the commander to consult with immediate direct reports as a group; they could outvote the commander's decision. His direct reports for Bering on the *St. Peter* were Sven Waxell, Andreas Hesselberg, and Safron Khitrovo who were members of the council, along with Vitus Bering. The members of the council had to document their decisions. The sea council was a double-edged sword during the expedition. The sea council met to review instructions from the imperial court and determine the direction to reach America by heading southeast. *St. Peter* would then follow the coastline to 65 degrees N and eventually return to Avacha Bay after staying the winter in America.

The *St. Peter* and *St. Paul* expeditions did not proceed as smoothly as envisioned. A supply vessel, called the *Nadezhda*, hit a sand bar and needed repairs, was under the command of Khitrovo; the vessel was to transport provisions to Avacha Bay. However, the provisions were transported overland by coercing natives, which resulted in a revolt and a massacre. By late September, all three vessels linked up with *St. Peter* and *St. Paul*, heading together to begin their exploration of the northern Pacific Ocean.

Sailing across the northern Pacific Ocean was as challenging, perhaps more so, than leading the expedition across Russia from St. Petersburg to Kamchatka. Mother nature presented dangers, some expected while others not. The *St. Peter* experienced shifting violent winds peppered with windless days, which resulted in sporadic progress and excessive tacking; the ocean pounded the decks and sometimes damaged the vessel with a relentless fury; the heavy overcasts often made it difficult to calculate the vessel's location for lengthy periods of time; snow, hail, sleet, and rain made the lives of the crew members miserable as they worked the decks and the rigging. If mother nature did not add enough troubles, the human condition did. Scurvy, not unique to expeditions of the time, struck the crew hard, striking the top of the command to the bottom. Occasionally, Bering engaged with natives, such as the Aleuts, which sometimes resulted in hostilities. The crew's view of the natives as "idolaters" did not make the encounter very pleasant. Finally, Bering and his crew were constantly pursuing freshwater, as the violent winds caused the *St. Peter* to seem to tack aimlessly across the northern Pacific while striving to return to homeport. If all this was not enough, conflict among the senior officers during sea councils whittled away the authority of Vitus Bering.

The trip was a tragedy in the making. The *St. Peter* and *St. Paul* had lost contact with one another despite the former trying to find the latter. In July 1741, Bering sighted the American continent, seeing the St. Elias Mountain Range. Bering felt that the conditions did not allow for landing. Instead, he headed toward Kayak Island to determine if it provided a safe harbor. Steller went ashore to make his observations about the natural environment.

Bering was now becoming nervous about not returning to Avacha Bay. Despite the severe shortage of water, he wanted to return due to the upcoming inclement weather. His decision conflicted with his senior officers, Waxell and Khitrovo, who wanted to continue the expedition. This difference was the beginning of a weakening of Bering's authority since members of the council overruled him. As a result, the vessel headed southwest rather than back to Avacha Bay. In the end, the council had clearly made a mistake. Another council meeting resulted in the decision to head north for water, passing the Shumagin Islands, and then return to Avacha Bay.

The loss of time, though, had jeopardized the opportunity to return to Kamchatka. Bering remained at odds with Waxell and Khitrovo.

The situation had become desperate. A decision was made to find a bay as they approached land, thinking it was Kamchatka, only to find out later that it was an island, destined to become Bering Island. Although Bering managed to issue orders, leadership had fallen upon Waxell and Steller. After a violent storm wrecked the *St. Peter* completely, the entire crew was now onshore in tents made from the vessel's sails. While the island had plenty of water, as well as animal and plant life, the ravages of scurvy had taken the lives of many crew members, including Vitus Bering, the commander of *St. Peter*. In the end, Bering had been right, if only the other members of the council had respected his authority.

Lessons

So, what are some of the key lessons (Figure 11.1) project managers can learn from Vitus Bering's experience on staying on track?

Understand the impact of changing sponsors. Vitus Bering had a major champion for his expedition, Peter the Great. Bering's expedition fell firmly into the vision of the tsar. Lucky for Bering, he also had the support, for the most part, of the Senate and Admiralty. However, the support of the Senate was tenuous at best, and the administrators for the expedition often exhibited a lack of cooperation, such as the one in Okhotsk, who was an exile from the court of Catherine I. Unfortunately for the expedition, Catherine I died, bringing Empress Anna Ivanova to power. Anna took some time to consolidate her power, which weakened sponsorship for the expedition. This weakened sponsorship led Bering to consider retirement.

Keep the overhead to a minimum. During the first and second expeditions, Bering's wagon trains were burdened with supplies and equipment, especially for building boats, barges, and bridges. Despite the enormous quantity, Bering did not have enough. He sent advance parties to meet with administrators in other cities to procure additional resources, often unsuccessfully. The lack of resource

The Lessons of Vitus Bering

- Understand the impact of changing sponsors
- Keep the overhead to a minimum
- Be aware of negative team dynamics
- Adapt to changing circumstances

Figure 11.1   The Lessons of Vitus Bering.

optimization resulted in delays in the expeditions as the wagon trains worked their way from St. Petersburg to Kamchatka. Also contributing to this challenge was a shortage of available funds. The lack of resource optimization led Bering to resort to negative measures to acquire what was needed for the expeditions, such as what occurred in Kamchatka.

Be aware of negative team dynamics. Almost from the start of the expeditions, tensions among team members arose. Professors complained incessantly because of their dashed expectations of their roles and perks on the expectations. Georg Steller, the naturalist on the second expedition, clashed with Bering. During the second expedition, members of the sea council overruled the Dane. Bering faced rebellion among his men in Okhotsk during the first expedition. During the second expedition, Bering sent a team of surveyors and soldiers to find a better route to the Sea of Okhotsk, only to learn that no one wanted to follow the orders of the surveyors. Even some of his sponsors accused him of cowardice because he did not continue north to determine whether a "bridge" existed between Asia and North America and did not conduct an exploration of the other. In the end, a breakdown in the unity of command killed Bering and many other members of his crew.

Adapt to changing circumstances. The expeditions were a prime example of failing to adapt. The fact that the natives were coerced into providing provisions and manpower and, consequently, rebelled demonstrated a desperation on the part of Bering and his officers to complete the missions. Rebellions by the natives and other Siberians occurred in Tobolsk, Yakutsk, and Okhotsk. The inability to resolve differences, such as in pursuit of freshwater and the route to Avacha Bay, among the senior officers also led to difficulties in adapting to changing circumstances, leading to inflexibility in decision-making and ending with the crew being marooned on Bering Island.

Final Thoughts

Vitus Bering was a foreigner in charge of other ones, being a Dane in a vessel with crew members from other nations, including from his adopted nation, Russia. He had the sponsorship from the czar and czarina; however, he lost the support of the former due to the czar's death and, for a long time, the czarina's until she had consolidated her power. Even with their support, Bering faced problems with stakeholders, whether they were members of his crew, governors, or members of the Russian Senate. The members of his council, which he was required to consult, overruled him; the council made subsequent decisions that Bering had to accept, which in the end proved he, not the council, was right. Bering was not adept at responding to unexpected circumstances, even when forced to stay on the island that would eventually be named after him. His logistical plan appeared impractical when it became clear he did not receive enough resources either from the Russian government or the governors. He frequently had trouble determining their heading and location, especially on the second expedition. As a result, they ended up on an island when they thought they were heading to Kamchatka.

Project managers not only need to know their vision and goals for their projects; they also need to know how well they are approaching each one. That requires taking frequent status regularly by collecting reliable and valid data to turn into information. Without that feedback, they will never know whether their projects are partially or fully complete. Project managers, often not of their choosing, need to consult with their leads, but the ultimate decision and responsibility for results lie with the former. Even during a power contest, project managers must stand their ground and not relinquish that responsibility as Bering did toward the end of his second expedition when his council overruled him on several occasions. The continued support of a powerful sponsor can prevent this type of circumstance from arising, which even the most seasoned project managers face in their careers.

Chapter 12

Meriwether Lewis and William Clark: Adapting to Change

Being able to adjust to changing conditions in a manner that enables achieving a goal.

Two men, Meriwether Lewis and William Clark, crossed the North American continent leading a group of soldiers and volunteers into a vast unknown that would someday result in the most productive, powerful nation in the history of the world. They would have to face devastating diseases like malaria, dysentery, and syphilis; wild animals, including bears and wolves; hostile tribes, such as the Sioux; turbulent waters with submerged trees and rocks just below the surface; inclement weather to include raging thunderstorms; unyielding insects like mosquitoes and gnats; and excruciating pain, such as from gunshot wounds and frostbite, all in an effort to satisfy the requirements of the third president of the United States, Thomas Jefferson. Their goals, as determined by the president, were as much scientific as they were commercial. If gold was involved, it was in the form of fur and the potential for trade among the Indians that occupied the vast lands of what became known as the Louisiana Purchase. The president also wanted to engender peace among the natives, more out of self-interest to establish trading posts. Of course, the discovery of a great water route through the northwest, anticipating the Missouri River being just that, would enhance commerce.

DOI: 10.1201/9781003028734-12

Background

Jefferson was a president of great intellect coupled with a sharp inquisitive mind, and Meriwether Lewis would be the means to satisfy it. Lewis, though not college educated, under the auspices of Jefferson underwent extensive education and training that prepared Lewis for the great expedition. Lewis, just like Jefferson, came from the patrician class of the Americans, and they were long acquainted with one another through the latter's father. After participating in the Whiskey Rebellion as a private in the Virginia militia and narrowly avoiding a court-martial offense as a junior officer, Lewis joined a group of sharpshooters commanded by William Clark.

Lewis received invaluable knowledge and experience of the frontier as it was known at the time. His military duties, especially as a paymaster, required him to travel throughout places like western Pennsylvania, the Carolinas, and the Ohio River Valley. Eventually, he was promoted to captain.

Clark was no less fortunate than Lewis. He came, too, from a preeminent family, his father being General George Rogers Clark who distinguished himself during the Revolutionary War. William Clark, too, would distinguish himself in the Battle of Fallen Timbers. Clark's military experience as an officer, being a captain, would serve him well during the expedition. He knew how to direct and lead men in the field and ensure that the team was ready to embark on and complete the expedition. In a sense, Clark was the practical commander in the field. Unfortunately, he had to leave the military due to financial problems with the family business.

Lewis, though practical in many regards, represented more the intellectual side of the expedition. As mentioned earlier, he had an immense intellectual curiosity, was a quick study, and had learned many of the requisite skills as a member of the American patricians, like horseback riding and hunting. He also had a unique ability to communicate and negotiate with a wide group of people, which would help him become even closer to Jefferson when Lewis became the president's aide de camp. This assignment helped solidify the relationship between the two men. Jefferson then selected Lewis (who was not his first choice) to lead the expedition. Lewis, in addition to planning for the expedition, was sent to Philadelphia, which was home to the American Philosophical Society. Lewis received an in-depth, expedited education on a wide range of topics that would serve him well during the expedition. He learned celestial navigation, botany, natural history, paleontology (especially dinosaur fossils), medical treatments, taxidermy, map reading, etc. During this intense learning period, he also endured the frustrations of ensuring the supplies and equipment were procured. These provisions included salted pork and beef, portable soup, salt, and medicines, such as opium, calomel, and ointments. The equipment included rifles and the accompanying powder and ammunition, compasses, woolen goods, paper, writing utensils, mosquito netting, tents, and candles. He also procured gifts for the Indians he would encounter along the way; these included mainly medals, beads, scissors; sewing items; knives; and many other trinkets and utilitarian items that the Indians might find of value. These goods were eventually distributed as a sign of friendship but also to exchange for food and horses. An interesting note was that he also worked on a collapsible boat that he and Jefferson designed for the expedition, which would cause him much consternation before the expedition was executed, causing a delay in the schedule.

Preparing plans for the expedition was quite impressive. Lewis worked closely with his sponsor, Thomas Jefferson, to identify and address planning details. Lewis received financial and political support from the president. They defined the goals of the expedition, as well as the training and resource requirements to succeed. They engaged the right subject matter experts, some from the American Philosophical Society, such as Dr. Benjamin Rush who created a mega stool softener called the "Thunder Clapper," and cartographers who developed maps and reviewed existing ones developed by other explorers—e.g., ones developed during Captain James Cook's expedition to the northwest.

Jefferson had a major request of Lewis. He wanted the young explorer to take plenty of notes. He wanted the captain to record all observations from a cultural and scientific perspective. He wanted Lewis to record information and insights about the Indians, including their physical characteristics, customs, weapons, diets, and relationships with other tribes. The president also wanted him to record the climate, terrain, flora, and fauna, not just for commercial purposes but also for scientific ones.

Clark had not yet arrived on the scene but soon did. A cardinal rule of military discipline is to always have a chain of command in place so that if the officer in charge is incapacitated or killed, another person can quickly assume command. The person of choice from the perspective of Lewis was William Clark. Although the two men had not known each other long, Lewis had high respect for and trust in the former captain of the sharpshooters; Clark felt the same about Lewis. Clark agreed to join the expedition. If not for the mutual trust and respect, having two leaders on the expedition could have caused serious trouble between the two. That did not happen. A major reason was that the two men's talents, capabilities, and personalities complemented one another. As mentioned earlier, Lewis had an inquisitive intellect that would satisfy the requirements of an equally intelligent president. Clark appears just as smart as Lewis. The primary difference was that Clark had more experience leading men under difficult circumstances and had excellent skills in developing maps for unknown areas like the Louisiana Territory. If something happened to Lewis, Clark would have no problem replacing him, perhaps other than from a scientific perspective.

Before the expedition formally began, Lewis leapfrogged from one location to another to get the necessary provisions. He went to Harper's Ferry, Philadelphia, and Pittsburgh. He also scrambled for manpower and supplies, even while progressing down the Ohio and Missouri Rivers. He was selective in the choice of the men for the expedition, looking for people with specific skills, not just as hunters, though important, but also interpreters who were familiar with French and Indian languages (to include sign language). The interpreters were traders who knew not just the terrain and languages but also the culture of many Indian tribes.

Selecting men for what would be called the Corps of Discovery started with some difficulty. He had visited forts to evaluate and select men he thought had the skills and character to endure the expedition. Clark also contributed toward the selection of the Corps. Some men, like all manpower selections, were not the right choice. He released a few men over disciplinary issues. Lewis and Clark, based upon their experience as military officers, knew that discipline was important, especially on this expedition where all members had to perform their roles and responsibilities; otherwise, certain behaviors could jeopardize the lives of others. These and other disciplinary problems surfaced during the expedition, especially at the beginning when the final count of 33 men entered the North American version of the heart of darkness, the Louisiana Territory.

Lewis, and Clark, as with all planning, could not anticipate everything they needed nor the events that would occur as they departed from St. Louis in 1804 until they reached the Oregon coast in 1805.

Situation

Before the expedition, the United States was still a young republic facing then three behemoth empires, England, Spain, and France, not to mention Russia. England, on the west coast, was a prevalent power engaged in the fur trade, especially north of the Louisiana Territory. Russia was in Oregon. Spain was south of the English on the west coast but the former also had possession of the Louisiana Territory until it was sold and transferred to France. Then, the French sold it to the United States for $15 million.

The United States knew little about the land it purchased from the French. Few if anybody knew the actual boundaries of the Louisiana Territory. That limited knowledge would change, of course, with the expedition of Lewis and Clark as they proceeded down the Ohio, Mississippi, Missouri, and Columbia rivers.

Expedition

The expedition required traveling to and from many locations, which are listed in the following two paragraphs. (Note that the first sequence is meant to be a high-level summary of locations going from east to west. The second sequence is a high-level summary of the return trip from west to east.)

From east to west: St. Louis (Missouri), Camp Dubois (Illinois), Kansas and Platte (Nebraska) Rivers, Camp Whitefish (Nebraska); Bluff (Nebraska); Calumet Bluff (Nebraska); Fort Mandan (North Dakota); Yellowstone River (North Dakota) Marias River (Montana); Great Falls (Montana); Three Forks (Montana);

Camp Fortunate (Montana), Lemhi Pass (Montana/Idaho), Bitterroot Mountains (Montana/Idaho), Lolo Hot Springs/Lolo Pass (Montana/Idaho), Clearwater River (Idaho), Snake River (Idaho), Columbia River (Washington/Oregon), and Pillar Rock (Washington), Fort Clatsop (Oregon).

From west to east: Fort Clatsop (Oregon), Willamette River (Oregon), Walla Walla (Washington), Celilo Falls (Oregon/Washington), Bitterroot Mountains (Idaho/Montana), Marias River (Montana)/Camp Fortunate (Montana), Yellowstone River (North Dakota), Missouri River (Montana/North Dakota), Fort Mandan (North Dakota), Cheyenne River (South Dakota), Vermillion River (South Dakota), Sioux City (Iowa), St. Charles (Missouri), Fort Bellefontaine (Missouri), and St. Louis (Missouri).

The Corps faced many challenges, and it managed to surmount many of them. Here are just some of the unanticipated challenges encountered during the expedition.

They had insufficient food or what they brought along became spoiled; other times, food was plentiful. The salted pork and beef, as well as portable soup, for example, could only serve their needs so much. They feasted on buffalo, elk, bear, and beavertail to supplement their diets, but sometimes even that food was unavailable and brought the Corps to near starvation. At some points, they resorted to eating horse flesh and dog, which Lewis grew quite fond of, minus eating his dog named Seaman. They supplemented their diet with wild vegetation, such as camas and Wapato roots, which often caused severe illness for many members of the Corps. Occasionally, they would reach points during their expedition when they hunted game, such as deer and elk, when the animals were plentiful, such as at Ft. Mandan or upon reaching a fork in the Missouri River. They also sent hunting parties to hunt game and shared their meat with the natives, like the Shoshonis. The prairie also presented amble game, such as buffalo, elk, deer, and geese, which kept the members of the Corps fed. Upon reaching the west coast, the Corps experienced serious problems with food. At Fort Clatsop, the humidity and rain caused elk meat to spoil, leading to illness. Hunting and fishing declined, forcing them to depart Fort Clatsop.

The range and magnitude of illnesses and injuries were challenging. Boils were a persistent problem among the men pulling the canoes and pirogues through the water; the boils were likely caused by the dirty water in which they waded. They also had frequent bouts of dysentery and constipation from the water and food. Some men contracted malaria from the wave of mosquitoes that attacked them, not to say anything about the swarm of gnats continuously encircling them. Some men contracted as well as spread venereal diseases to the natives. Gunshot wounds plagued members on the expedition, including ones from within the ranks, which included Lewis accidentally being shot by a private. The natives, too, suffered from many diseases, such as rheumatism and eye infections. Lewis applied his medical training to help, for example, the Shoshonis, and this service also helped to barter for food and horses; this service also helped to build goodwill with the tribes.

Traveling the Missouri River became a challenge in several ways. Certain points in the river were so shallow or filled with rocks and debris that they had to portage the vessels, meaning they had to carry the vessels on land, usually along the bank of the river. Other times, the men had to pole the vessels or pull them through the water. Sometimes the expedition proceeded down the Missouri River and encountered a fork. Lewis and Clark had to send an advance party to determine which branch was the Missouri River. The wrong choice could jeopardize the expedition. Lewis and Clark, however, did not just rely on the advance party. For example, they obtained information from the natives, such as the Hidatsas and the Mandans, about which river to take. They crosschecked the information that they had received with other Indian tribes to help determine its reliability.

Some men, too, became a challenge. This challenge arose more at the beginning of the expedition rather than later. Once they reached the truly unknown parts of the expedition, such as upon departing from Ft. Mandan, the men had no choice but to work together; however, even then, disciplinary problems arose. In the early time of the expedition, some men fought with one another or disregarded the orders of a sergeant. Some men raided the whiskey supply or caused some disruption within the ranks with negative talk about Lewis and Clark, fell asleep at the post, and another deserted. If someone was not released from the expedition, they might receive a lashing. Physical punishment was not the only means to instill discipline. They implemented military drills to ensure every man knew his assigned responsibilities, assigned sentries, and announced, so to speak, their marching orders. These especially became critical when exploring uncharted areas. From that point onward, the disciplinary problems decreased dramatically.

Related to manpower, Lewis and Clark had to continuously search for qualified men while traveling along the Mississippi and Missouri Rivers; they were still short-staffed for men who could man the keelboat. They were also short of interpreters. Fortunately, the St. Louis area had French fur traders, such as George Drouillard, who knew some natives' languages and had knowledge about or experience with the Missouri River. The legendary Sacagawea, a wife of the trader Toussaint Charbonneau, who joined the expedition while the Corps established Ft. Mandan, was a Shoshoni who was captured by the Hidatsas. She and Charbonneau proved invaluable as interpreters during the expedition; Sacagawea was also proved invaluable in procuring horses from the Shoshonis, the tribe from which she was abducted. Lewis and Clark would also bring on board two new soldiers of mixed native and white descent who functioned as guides and interpreters. Lewis and Clark also tapped the knowledge and linguistic expertise of traders who lived among certain tribes, like John Gravelines and Pierre-Antoine Tabeau living among the Arikaras. Lewis and Clark had also the assistance of the Nez Perce and Shoshonis when traveling the Columbia River.

Another challenge that impacted the kickoff of the expedition was the delayed transfer of the Louisiana Territory over to the United States. The Spanish still held possession and had transferred it to the French to complete the exchange. Then, once the French received possession of the territory, it was transferred to the United States. This series of transfers caused a delay due to the diplomatic formalities. As a result, the expedition spent a winter outside St. Louis at what became known as Camp Dubois. Despite the delay, Lewis and Clark turned the situation into an opportunity. They obtained additional men and supplies, as well as built esprit de corps. Lewis took longitude and latitude measurements, developed questionnaires to collect and compile information from locals, and prepared his speech to native tribes.

The relationships among the tribes presented a challenge. Many of the tribes were antagonistic toward one another. Jefferson ordered Lewis and Clark to try to build not only good relations with each tribe but also among the tribes, which proved no easy accomplishment. One of their attempts to bring peace was to implement councils; in theory, the chiefs had appeared to resolve their differences internally and externally. Some councils went well; other times, they did not, such as the one with the Teton Sioux. The mixed success of the councils was due largely to tribes fighting among one another, such as the Otos, Mandans, Arikaras, Hidatsas, Yanktons, Sioux, Shoshoni, Flatheads, Nez Perce, and Blackfeet, among others. For example, the tension among the Sioux, Hidatsas, Mandans, and Arikaras was especially complex. The Mandans tried to keep the Hidatsas away from the Corps to monopolize the trade with the expedition. The Sioux joined with the Arikaras and attacked the Mandans. The Shoshonis and the Blackfeet were enemies. When the Nez Perce guided the Corps, they decided to leave the expedition after revealing that the tribe was at war with the Wishram-Wasco tribes. Some tribes were also suspicious that the Corps was working in concert with another tribe, such as with the Omahas against the Teton Sioux. Even the Shoshonis, the original tribe of Sacagawea, were initially suspicious of the Corps, thinking that the white men were helping the Blackfeet entrap them.

The weather and the terrain were constant challenges. As the Corps proceeded down the Missouri River and approached the mouth of the Kansas River, a rising river with floating debris and severe winds impeded their progress, and rainstorms soaked their clothes, food, and guns. The Corps also faced severe winter weather going through the Bitterroot Mountains and the Cascades, both a part of the Rockies. The men faced frostbite and a lack of meat to increase their endurance when carrying equipment and supplies; the bitter cold made game unavailable. At Fort Clatsop, the weather was particularly uncomfortable due to the constant rain, high humidity, fog, and cloudiness. Some men suffered from severe colds and rheumatism.

The terrain presented challenges, too. The fork as they approached the Great Falls required choosing between a north fork and the other south fork. Lewis sent scouting parties up each one, ultimately selecting the south fork. The information from the Hidatsas helped them to navigate the south fork by noting that only the pirogues and canoes could make it through the falls. Even then the Corps had to reduce the number of vessels, resorting to portaging and laying caches to lighten the load. The trek through the Great Falls was brutal, especially for those who were portaging. The prickly pears and rocks tore at the flesh of their feet, and they were consequently fatigued. To add to the challenge, as they passed through the falls and entered a valley, the Corps spotted another fork consisting of three rivers, mountains in a distance, and a column of smoke, a signal by natives, the Shoshonis, warning them to retreat. Lewis and Clark, the latter sick, decided to build a fort at what became known as the Three Forks. This time provided an opportunity for the Corps to rest, heal, hunt game and collect other edibles, and build and repair clothing made of animal skins. While Clark stayed at the fort, Lewis, along with a few members of the Corps, went in search of the Shoshonis, whom they encountered.

Lessons

So, what are some of the key lessons (Figure 12.1) project managers can learn from Lewis and Clark's experience of embracing the unknown?

Understand planning is useful only up to a certain point. Jefferson and Lewis knew they had a major challenge ahead. The United States was vast even before the expedition, but the president had his sights on the country becoming bigger. Jefferson, along with his aide de camp, planned extensively. Jefferson and Lewis determined manpower and equipment requirements, identified the necessary training for Lewis, designated the potential pathway to the west coast, clarified expectations, and equipment needs. Jefferson, in conversations and letters, also articulated the goals of the expedition, which, of course, helped to determine requirements. However, Jefferson and Lewis knew that such an expedition could not be planned in toto. Too many unknowns existed. A few examples that surfaced were the problems and delays associated with developing the keelboat and the transportation problems with delivering rifles identified to Philadelphia, or the difficulties with

The Lessons of Lewis and Clark

- Understand that planning is useful only up to a certain point
- Recognize each stakeholder is different
- Strive for strong sponsorship
- Expect the environment to always change; nothing is static
- Remember esprit de corps is a key element of success
- Address disciplinary issues early
- Solicit help from various stakeholders
- Take risks but do so intelligently
- Learn to speak each stakeholder's language
- Build a strong relationship with all stakeholders

Figure 12.1 The Lessons of Lewis and Clark.

determining which river was the Missouri when encountering forks, such as what occurred at Three Forks. Lewis and Clark adjusted plans to adapt to the changing environment, such as sending scouting parties ahead of the rest of the Corps to ascertain whether to proceed on the same route or take a different one.

Recognize each stakeholder is different. Like other explorers, Lewis and Clark often treated the indigent population as monolithic in terms of their needs and even culture. The two explorers discovered that was not the case. The tribes often varied in their needs and expectations. Beads and medals were popular with the Mandans, but these and other presents did not meet the expectations of the Teton Sioux. Since they traded with the Spanish and the English, the Siouxs' expectations of the Americans were much grander. After all, the English traded guns, which many Indian tribes considered as having greater value than what the expedition offered. Even when the Corps was at Ft. Clatsop, the expectations of the natives, such as the Chinook, were much higher than what the Corps had to offer. The offerings were even more problematic, even insulting, to some tribes on the west coast. Lewis and Clark also discovered at their councils that the Indians were different culturally and that animosity existed among them, even after agreeing to make peace. Finally, some natives were more prosperous than others, thanks in part to the wars among the tribes, such as the Hidatsas who were wealthier than the poorer Shoshonis. Lewis and Clark were less than successful in bringing about peace. Lewis gave the standard speech and offered the same presents, acting as if one-size-fits-all, which was incorrect.

Strive for strong sponsorship. Not everyone was thrilled about the expedition from a political perspective. For example, the differences between Jefferson and the Federalists over the expedition could have become worse. Jefferson provided the political and financial support for the expedition when dealing with Congress. He also kept engaged with Lewis's progress regarding the expedition, from start to finish. He wanted to see results so that he would not only counter the concerns expressed by the Federalists but also continue to receive support from the American Philosophical Society in Philadelphia. Lewis and Clark led the Corps without having to worry about losing Jefferson's support.

Expect the environment to always change; nothing is static. The expedition constantly faced a changing environment. The climate often oscillated between extreme heat during the day and cold at night. The winds, too, became mercurial; they might provide a steady or no breeze or transform into a turbulence threatening to capsize a pirogue or canoe, resulting in a loss of food, equipment, life, and specimens; such circumstances arose on the Columbia River. The Missouri presented many challenges, too, when some parts of the river were shallow and other parts filled with subsurface debris. There were also rapids, such as at Great Falls and the Snake and Clearwater Rivers that could potentially cause loss. The variability in the terrain raised the stakes. The Corps experienced, for example, prairies, Bitterroot Mountains, and the Great Divide. The Corps did whatever was necessary to navigate the environment.

Remember esprit de corps is a key element of success. Lewis and Clark recognized the need to engender esprit de corps among the team. In the beginning, engendering it was not easy as people, soldiers and volunteers, gradually joined the Corps. Lewis and Clark held celebrations for key moments like Christmas and Independence Day. They allowed periodic "parties," which would include music and dancing either as a separate team or with the natives, such as they did with the Mandans, Shoshonis, and even the Teton Sioux. They also delegated tasks so that members of the Corps acquired a sense of ownership in the outcome as they did when exploring which of the rivers to take when encountering forks. By trying to keep the esprit de corps high, soldiers and volunteers alike were more alert, worked better together, and prepared themselves when entering the unknown, like after departing from Fort Mandan.

Address disciplinary issues early. Closely tied with esprit de corps is the issue of discipline. Without discipline, people find it difficult to work with one another, especially under intense and ambiguous situations like what the Corps experienced. In the beginning, the Corps experienced quite a few disciplinary problems. Soldiers deserted, were insubordinate toward sergeants, became drunk, suggested mutiny, and fought with one another. The captains knew they had to introduce discipline if the expedition was to succeed, especially when entering unknown, hostile territory. Members of the Corps needed to have rules and know the penalties for violating them. They held court-martials, banished some men, and even administered lashings. Lewis and Clark needed everyone to understand and follow the rules to deal with tense situations, as was the case when confronting the Teton Sioux. As the team progressed into the unknown territory, disciplinary issues declined.

Solicit help from various stakeholders. Lewis and Clark saw the value of engaging with the chiefs of the native tribes, from the Mandans and Hidatsas to the Shoshonis and the Sioux. They recognized the chiefs knew the terrain, location of other Indian tribes, and the complex relationships among the tribes. They also sought information from traders that lived among the tribes, such as Pierre-Antoine Tabeau who lived among the Arikawas. Soliciting information from all relevant parties proved especially valuable as the Corps traversed the Columbia River and met with other tribes, such as the Walla Walla, Wishram, and Chinook. The Indians that they met earlier accompanied the expedition as guides because the Corps lacked an understanding of the language and culture of the Pacific coast tribes; the Nez Perce guides revealed they were enemies of the Wishram-Wasco Indians and left the Corps.

Take risks but do so intelligently. Going on the expedition that Lewis and Clark took required tremendous courage due to the known and unknown risks that they could and did face. They did not, however, take foolish risks, even when presented with some unanticipated issues. When they encountered forks in the river, they sent scouting parties to collect and verify information that the route they took had a good probability of being the right one. Such was the case when encountering the Three Forks. They also sent advance parties to determine whether they would encounter any problems, such as shoals or rapids, and did the same when traveling through the Great Falls by determining the best means to navigate it. They also recognized when they wanted to take a shortened approach, such as when they departed from Ft. Clatsop. They did so only after listening to the chief of the Walla Walla tribe who told them of a shortcut to the Clearwater River.

Learn to speak each stakeholder's language. The natives did not speak a common tongue, and the Corps continually had problems in this regard. However, Lewis and Clark knew what they needed—interpreters. Many of the fur traders spoke a European language, such as French, Spanish, or English in addition to one or more native languages and a sign language that was common among the tribes. Also, some soldiers, especially ones who were called "half-breeds," spoke both English and a native language. Sacagawea also provided invaluable language skills, being a Shoshoni and living among the Hidatsas. Sometimes the translations involved several individuals translating, for example, English into French and then into a native American language, and then the process reversed itself, which had the potential to turn into a misinterpretation. A linguistic problem arose when the Corps entered the Pacific west coast, where even the Indians accompanying them could not speak or understand the language, such as that spoken by the Chinook.

Build a strong relationship with all stakeholders. A solid relationship with all involved parties is invaluable, especially if built from having mutual interests and trust. Lewis and Clark, under the direction of Jefferson, wanted to establish not only good relationships among the tribes but also with the Corps. The captains not only dispensed gifts, albeit some tribes were disappointed like the Teton Sioux, but also went on joint hunts, visited the villages, and watched and even joined in on the dances and celebrations. They also shared food from the hunts, such as with the Shoshonis, and Lewis applied his medical training to address illnesses afflicting many Native Americans.

Final Thoughts

Meriwether Lewis and William Clark supported one another on their expedition. They achieved something few expeditions deployed successfully: two people in charge working harmoniously throughout the expedition. They seemed to complement one another in terms of personality, and their responsibilities were divided up accordingly. Despite all their planning, especially on the part of Jefferson and Lewis, they knew they were entering the unknown and could not anticipate everything. That did not mean they failed to prepare themselves in a way that would enable them to adapt to their environment. One important way that enabled them to adapt was having the wisdom and strength to talk with people to obtain and crosscheck information that would help them identify which tribes to invite to councils and their relationship with one another; they also conversed about the best routes to take during their expedition. When they lacked reliable information, such as when encountering a fork and deciding which branch to take, the other approach taken was to send scouting parties to collect the necessary information to decide which one to pursue.

Most project managers never have a sponsor at the level of a president, nor did they ever have to experience the challenges, risks, and obstacles of a Lewis and Clark when entering a territory unmapped and filled with potential enemies. But they have experienced some of the same challenges. These include training people quickly to perform efficiently and effectively, having adequate resources on hand, trying to resolve differences among stakeholders, dealing with constant change and unanticipated events, and even disciplinary problems. Project managers have also experienced the value of working closely with stakeholders to understand their needs and wants, to speak their language, and to support one another in achieving goals, all of which enable them to adapt to change.

Chapter 13

Ernest Shackleton: Leading

Providing to a team the necessary direction and guidance to achieve a vision or goal.

Imagine leading a group of men into the frigid Antarctic.

Suddenly the ship is squeezed like a pimple by two ice floes. The wooden deck and planks begin to crack and buckle. The water squirts between each plank and shoots at them like lasers as the vessel lists. Men and dogs, along with supplies, provisions, and equipment, slide across the deck as if on a shuffleboard. The stern of the vessel is lifted skyward as the bow goes in the opposite direction. The men onboard struggle to work the bilge pumps to keep the vessel from descending into the bowels of the ice. The sounds of cracking ice and a vessel being smashed become indistinguishable.

The men rush to unload the supplies, provisions, equipment, and themselves off the vessel that took them to the Antarctic and was to return them to their home-port. But the ice keeps crushing the vessel like a tin can, as even more water rushes into the bilge and storage areas, threatening to drown some men in just a matter of minutes; the ship is becoming their coffin.

The men hurry to unload the ship, facing unimaginable circumstances. The wind blows more than 50 miles per hour whipping their faces as the flakes from a blizzard strike everyone like bullets from a machine gun. The snow on the ice pack or a floe beneath their feet gives a false sense of security, not realizing that a crack can occur anytime and swallow them like a swimmer hunted by a great white shark.

Soon, most of what they need is at a base camp but not everything. Tents are pitched and the huskies are secure. Everyone is relieved that they will survive and believes that it is just a matter of time before the floe will loosen its grip, and they can reload their ship and in a matter of months continue their mission. Then one day, they watch as their vessel is swallowed by the ice and along with it their hopes.

If all this is not enough, hell breaks loose when the floe splits; the men scurry to their sledges and smaller boats and manage to escape just in time. The headway to a safe location goes slowly. Men find themselves fatigued and exhausted, the temperatures drop to unimaginable levels, causing frostbite, some develop dysentery and others have severe cases of constipation, Some men begin to argue with one another as tensions and fear begin to spread. Food can last for 90 days, no more. The darkness of the night arrives earlier and lasts longer.

You call an all-hands meeting. The 27 men look at you, wondering what happens next and how you are going to return them to safety. After all, they came on the expedition because of you and the adventure.

Welcome to Ernest Shackleton.

Background

Ernest Shackleton was not an amateur explorer when he arrived in Antarctica. He had been to the continent two times previously. Both experiences had prepared him for such a moment as described in the introduction.

His first trip to Antarctica was led by Captain Robert Scott. Shackleton was one of his lieutenants. In many respects, the expedition, formally called the National Antarctic Expedition, failed, but it did manage to go farther toward the South Pole than anyone previously. While Shackleton was liked by the men, he was not very well admired by Captain Scott, who thought Shackleton was temperamental, disobedient, and neglectful of some duties. Shackleton went as part of a small team, led by Scott, to the South Pole, which was never reached. Shackleton's health deteriorated from scurvy, a persistent cough, and leg pain. But Scott seemed to imply that Shackleton was a malingerer, contributing little to pulling the sledges and was sent to New Zealand. Perhaps Scott was retaliating for having been forced to take on Shackleton by one of the benefactors of the expedition.

Regardless of the first experience, Shackleton decided to return to Antarctica in 1908. He was determined to reach the South Pole. The original plan was to travel via the Ross Barrier, but he changed plans by taking a different route. The expedition experienced difficulties when the ponies pulling the sledges died and food supplies dwindled while crossing the Beardmore Glacier. The expedition was not a failure, having surpassed the spot where Captain Scott had ceased continuing farther.

His previous experiences obviously had an impact on him. His outstanding leadership qualities were exhibited during the third expedition. Before delving into the third expedition, which also ended in frustration and disappointment, here is some background about the man who would become an exemplar of leadership during a crisis.

Shackleton, born in 1874, came from a middle-class, Anglo-Irish family. His father, Henry, was a doctor, but young Ernst had no desire to enter the medical profession. He grew up in a large family, with Ernest being the oldest son. Perhaps the biggest influence on his character was his mother, Henrietta, who was optimistic, unpretentious, and a self-confident person, three qualities inculcated in him that would serve him well during his third expedition.

The family moved from an agricultural environment to Dublin. Eventually, he attended Dulwich College. However, he found college not to his liking, finding it tedious, something not suited to a young man who longed for adventure and had a vivid imagination. His performance as a student was not exceptional, and, due to his independent streak, he did not participate in sports. He initially thought about becoming a cadet with the British navy, but his father could not afford it; instead, Ernest settled for the merchant marine, eventually becoming an officer.

The background begs the question, What type of person was Ernest Shackleton? Answering this question reveals much about a man's capability to lead a crew through a crisis like the third expedition.

To some, this earlier Shackleton was loud, temperamental, and self-centered. He was often accused of being a womanizer, impulsive, theatric, and whimsical; others described him as being purposeful and goal oriented. To others, he was godlike, especially to the men whom he led to safety during the third expedition. He was considered by many on the third expedition as being considerate, approachable, and cared deeply about the welfare of his men while at the same time engendering respect by just about everyone on the crew. It is said that the true character of a man is revealed by how well he responds to a crisis. The evidence indicates that he had shed some of the negative characteristics of his younger years. His experiences leading up to the third expedition had obviously changed him, except perhaps for his temper. Even then, he managed to control it for the most part. He did retain the qualities he acquired from his mother: optimistic, unpretentious, and self-confident. By the time he was in his 40s, he had learned a great deal about leadership, especially during a crisis.

Situation

Back in the early 1900s, the last vestiges of discovery centered on principally two areas of the globe: the Arctic and Antarctica. The two areas were largely unexplored, spared by the ravages of colonialism. True, parts of Africa, Asia, and South America remained a mystery, but the northern and southern tips of the planet remained largely unexplored. Several attempts to explore the frigid areas of the globe were made during the 1800s, which often resulted in calamity for many expeditions. No one had yet made it to the very top and bottom of the world, however. The Americans and Europeans made attempts, but all resulted in partial success. Shackleton was determined to join the ranks of the explorers who would achieve what other men failed to accomplish, but, ironically, he suffered the same fate. What made him famous was how he dealt with the failure: bringing back all his men alive. His fame came from failure, perhaps as much as John Franklin's did when searching for the Northwest Passage, only Franklin suffered a worse fate: death.

Expedition

Shackleton managed to acquire the necessary financing for what was formally called the Imperial Trans-Antarctic Expedition from a wealthy Scotsman named Sir James Caird with additions from the Royal Geographical Society, and the government. He also leveraged his publications, photography, and commercial exploits to secure the financing. As the *Endurance* was being retrofitted for the expedition and rechartered, Shackleton interviewed potential candidates using what some would say were unorthodox approaches. He looked for men who would have no compunction toward taking on many tasks, some of them deemed menial. He also looked for potential team players with a mixture of experience. These characteristics would exist among most of the men who would eventually join the expedition regardless of whether they were engineers, navigators, seamen, photographers, artists, carpenters, meteorologists, surgeons, or physicists. Above all, they had to have a strong sense of loyalty, and Shackleton had to have a good sense of intuition about them.

Shackleton also knew the value of having an overall strategic plan. He developed one based on his previous experiences in Antarctica. He would take a ship to the Weddell Sea whereupon it would land a sledging party of six men and dogs, not ponies, and proceed to the South Pole. A second ship would approach McMurdo Sound in the Ross Sea and deploy caches within the vicinity of the South Pole. The sledging party from the Weddell Sea, after having reached the South Pole, would advance toward the Beardmore Glacier and eventually arrive at the base camp at McMurdo Sound. Simple enough; unfortunately, mother nature decided to interfere.

After departing London in 1914 during the initial start of World War I, the expedition proceeded toward Buenos Aires. At the Brazilian city, a few men had exhibited what he considered flaws, and he dismissed them and hired additional men, along with the delivery of approximately 70 dogs. From Buenos Aires, the expedition proceeded to South Georgia Island and the South Sandwich Islands. The *Endurance* gradually encountered pack ice, spotted large icebergs, and then found itself trapped in the ice of the Weddell Sea.

Shackleton established watches to spot an opportunity to break the ship free from the choking ice, but to no avail. Multiple attempts were made, despite maddening efforts by the men to chisel and saw the ice away and pulling chunks away. No success. The large floe carried the vessel toward Vahsel Bay. Suffice it to say, they were now captives.

Despite the dismal situation, Shackleton and the crew remained optimistic. Both on the *Endurance* and on the floe they tried to adapt, to be cautious, and to have "fun" at the same time. The quarters on the vessel were changed to provide more comfort and preclude them from sleeping outside in the minus teens or colder. Shackleton ensured that the men were adequately fed, allowing the men to hunt for blubber and meat. The huskies were moved from the *Endurance* to the floe; igloos were built to house the animals. Shackleton was not just concerned about the physical needs of the men, although he often placed a high priority on those needs for his crew. He was also concerned with their mental state. The daylight hours decreased and were replaced by the corresponding long nights. Prolonged darkness and the extreme cold had the potential to cause the men to fall into a deep depression and with that engender discord within the team. Shackleton placed an importance on engaging the men in activities to keep their minds off their situation. He would allow the photographer to show pictures, hold celebrations on notable calendar dates, offer toasts with a mug of grog, have sledge races, and play sports.

While the crew took an apparent respite, mother nature had other thoughts. The weather erupted into a blizzard and temperatures plummeted. The winds did not help, accelerating to 50 or more miles per hour, smothering one side of the vessel and scarring the other. Then came a loud cracking sound. The ice floe was breaking up, or so they thought. The men moved into action. The dogs and sledges were brought aboard the *Endurance*. The men waited for the floe to split apart. But no break, this time.

Despite the situation calming, the men remained nervous, realizing a crack could come at any time. They could not sleep due to the loud noises of the ice and ship breaking into pieces. The crack, or at least the sound of one, did, however, arrive. The pressure of the ice was crushing the *Endurance*.

The ship was floating in a body of water appearing on the starboard side of the ship. Shackleton tried to turn the situation into an opportunity by using the *Endurance* to force the crack wider, but to no avail; the floe trapped the vessel once again. The vessel listed, sliding just about everything in that direction. Eventually, the ship righted itself.

The situation seemed to have stabilized or so they thought once again. The pressure returned with a vengeance, impacting the bow, starboard, and stern of the *Endurance*. Shackleton ordered the dogs and sledges onto the vessel in case an opportunity for departure arose. Then he required the men to keep the pumps running but the effort failed. The ship continued snapping and cracking like the ice. As the situation subsided, the men pitched their tents, but the crack in the floe continued. Shackleton worried the base camp would split in two, separating the men. Unable to sleep, he felt the floe shake violently and had the men wakened. The *Endurance* began to fall apart, losing its bowsprit and jib boom.

Shackleton realized the status quo was unacceptable; not doing anything was a nonexistent part of his personality nor how he dealt with such circumstances. He eventually called an all-hands meeting to announce a plan, which was to lead the expedition to Paulette Island, a considerable distance away. He then restricted what the men could take with them and the quantity, with the expressed purpose of reducing weight. He then gave a pep talk and demonstrated he was willing to discard his valuables to reduce what he had to carry, an effort to set the example.

The men departed with Shackleton and three others in the lead. Their sledges carried tools, such as axes, to use to prepare hummocks so that the other sledges and crew could navigate over the hills. The distance traveled was painstakingly slow and physically exhausting; Shackleton limited the distance at any one time to travel to avoid the crew being separated by a major crack in the floe. Some men rode the sledges being pulled by the dogs; others pulled two of the three smaller vessels (the *James Caird, Dudley Docker,* and *Stancom Wills*) that were carried on the *Endurance.* Shackleton was displeased with the progress and decided to allow the floe to do the traveling; the only problem was the floe could proceed in any direction. He set up base camp and sent a team to return to the vessel to cannibalize what was left on board, as well as return with the third smaller vessel. Then another trip was taken to bring back anything else of value, especially food.

The impact on the men seemed to not diminish their optimism despite the setbacks. The potential for the floe to continue to break up and endanger them remained a real possibility. The weather and the inactivity could engender a sense of complacency and cause morale and esprit de corps to decline along with fluctuating temperatures. The temperature changes added difficulty in walking on the floe, softening in spots. Shackleton established a daily routine coupled with entertainment. He also assigned responsibilities now that they were no longer on the *Endurance,* ranging from who was responsible for each of the boats and the sledges. Meantime, the floe moved slowly as the crew's morale and esprit de corps started inevitably to decline. The situation could turn explosive among the men at any time. The inaction was affecting them.

Shackleton held an all-hands meeting and discussed the need to make more progress by traveling west in the smaller vessels, after sending a team to survey the possibility. The men pulled the *James Caird* into the water as a test case and across to a ridge and did likewise for the *Dudley Docker.* The next day, the crew formed a "wagon train" of sledges and boats and headed west; trudging through melted and refrozen snow, which proved treacherous and exhausting, especially for the men pulling the boats over ridges. The struggle continued into the next day. One of the men became insubordinate, which Shackleton addressed right away; the significance of the incident was that the team was starting to crack like the floe.

The expedition sought refuge on a more stable floe, settling on it for several days. Not unexpectedly, the morale and esprit de corps of the crew began to decline even more as the realization hit them that they may not extricate themselves from their situation. Wet clothes and limited rations, along with the climatic conditions, could not help but have a negative impact.

The dogs became a major concern. They were needed to pull the sledges. But the wet snow lessened their value, and they were now viewed more as a source of meat as the food supplies dwindled. Many of the dogs had deteriorated, too, from intestinal problems. The warm weather also caused the floe to soften and would pose a problem in trying to keep the dogs alive on the vessels. Shackleton gave the order to kill the dogs—a decision not well taken by the crew.

One would think that the warmer weather would boost morale and esprit de corps. But that was not the case. Traveling through the wet snow made movement more difficult. The danger of cracks separating the men and falling into the ocean increased their nervousness. Yet, the ice pack did not break apart, but the floe moved erratically. Boredom and disillusionment among the men increased. Their clothes, boots, and sleeping bags became drenched from water and the sweat of their bodies. The temperatures within the tents also increased, wetting their sleeping bags even further. The wind ran unabated, making it difficult to talk with one another or listen even to themselves. The men fell into greater depths of disillusionment and resignation. The men also had too much time available simply waiting without any sense of purpose except thinking about all their negative experiences and what they could face in the future. Their prospects looked bleak. The health of the men began to deteriorate, thanks largely to a diet of meat and blubber.

Not doing anything was out of the question. The long periods of inactivity were already generating hostility among the men. Shackleton then sent men back to a previous base camp to salvage any remaining food and other provisions; eventually, the *Stancomb Wills*, which had been left behind, rejoined the expedition.

The food began to dwindle fast despite measures being in place to limit the size of rations; seals and penguins were becoming fewer in number. Most of the rations were served cold because blubber used as fuel was dwindling and rations becoming smaller. The thoughts of cannibalism, supposedly mentioned in jest, were a topic of discussion. Some men became eerily silent.

One morning, the ominous crack occurred, the result of an ocean swell. The men scrambled about, noticing that they had been separated from food supplies, but they were able to retrieve the provisions. The men anticipated another opening to occur, but it did not occur right away. When a swell caused a significant crack in the floe, the men seemed to become complacent and then reacted; Shackleton took control and had the three vessels ready to go.

The floe continued to move about erratically due to the mercurial wind. Shackleton, after reviewing readings by the captain of the *Endurance*, determined that they should aim for King George Island rather than Clarence or Elephant Island. However, the wind was too erratic to have any assurance that would be the destination. The floe continued to split, separating the men from provisions and one of the vessels. Shackleton, nevertheless, decided to act by departing the floe.

Shackleton took the lead in the *James Caird* with the other two boats following. The crew was now facing a new set of problems. The sea waves rocked the boats, causing the men to jettison vital food and tools to evenly distribute the weight and preclude swamping. They also experienced the icy winds against their faces. The conditions became so unbearable that the vessels sought the protection of the side of an iceberg that was positioned away from the wind; the vessels were secured through lines and oars. The trouble with the decision was that it became a Catch-22 situation. The men camped on the iceberg, only to become the target of the wind and falling snow and ice. The men bivouacked for a night and then proceeded onward until they tethered themselves to a floe; however, Shackleton decided to shift the target from Clarence Island and Elephant Island to King George Island after discovering that they had ventured farther away from land, despite the route posing the danger of colliding with ice. The wind, however, often led them astray from their new destination. The destination changed again, and as their location shifted, the destination changed even again, this time back to Elephant Island.

Constant hunger, the freezing cold, sleeplessness, thirstiness, frostbite, and just pure physical exhaustion clobbered the physical well-being of the men, not to mention the giant swells threatening to sink their vessels. With the arrival of the nights, the terror continued. The men could not sleep; the danger of colliding with unseen ice increased the tension; the temperatures dropped; their clothing froze, not to mention themselves. Men began hoarding things for no reason while others cursed one another or wept. Men found themselves in deep cold water without anywhere to lay down. The vessels themselves were painted with thick ice, weighing them down and probably shifting the center of gravity.

Soon Clarence Island and Elephant Island appeared, but the men's and vessels' conditions did not improve. The vessels were covered in ice, and the men were a physical wreck. Shackleton ordered the men to prepare the vessels; they headed toward Elephant Island. The approach was not easy, and the *Dudley Docker* got separated from the other vessels but linked up eventually after much anguish and hostility among its crew. The vessels did not fare much better during the whole ordeal. Eventually, Shackleton spotted a position on the island, albeit narrow, for the men from all the vessels to land. The men enjoyed a respite and hunted for food; however, the respite was temporary. Shackleton noticed that the area was vulnerable to high tides and storms; they could not remain for long.

The vessels departed the next day based upon the observations made by Shackleton and his crew on the *Stancomb Wills*, which had found a safe place replete with seals, penguins, and other animals, as well as ice to melt for water. Boats progressed to the other side of the island, hugging the shore. As the vessels reached the location, the *Dudley Docker* strayed, but it soon worked its way back.

The shore was a spit with winds whipping man and land alike. The rocks provided little protection from the wind, along with blizzards. Nevertheless, the men had no other choice but to establish a base camp.

Shackleton then told the crew that he was going to lead a five-man party to travel 800 miles to South Georgia to secure their rescue. Shackleton cannibalized some of the other boats to reinforce the structure of the *James Caird*. He also took some of the food, clothing, equipment, and other provisions from the team left behind.

The journey was not a pleasant one for the six men heading to South Georgia. Besides the wind and the freezing temperature, the swells of the sea threatened to swamp or capsize the boat and, especially at night, the potential for colliding with ice was always present. The frostbite, waterlogged legs and feet, and exhaustion continued unabated. The situation was now one of man against the sea. If that was not enough, the men had to continuously bail water or shift the ballast. When able to sleep, they did so in wet, rotting sleeping bags and on top of the rocks sliding from side to side beneath them. The *James Caird* was smothered in ice, posing a danger to the buoyancy of the vessel and at one point a large wave nearly sank it. Ironically, quantities of fresh-water were declining, making reaching South Georgia a do-or-die situation.

Fortunately, the weather had improved. While the worry over water continued, Shackleton had another fear: accidentally bypassing South Georgia, which did not happen. Shackleton spotted a cove on South Georgia. Approaching the island proved challenging, but they were able to land after riding the combers; the landing was rough and damaged the vessel. The reality hit Shackleton; he and two other men had to travel across the island to seek help at Leith Harbor. Shackleton left three men behind with the wreckage of the *James Caird*. Shackleton and the two men took the minimum food and equipment to survive the trek. The men endured hardships of a different and similar nature from what they experienced at sea. Fog. Crevasses. Steep descents. Backtracking after realizing they were unable to travel farther. Falling asleep in the cold snow. Then they spotted Stromness Bay and, in a short time, rappelled themselves to their destination.

Lessons

So, what are some key lessons (Figure 13.1) project managers can learn from the experience of Ernest Shackleton on leading?

The Lessons of Ernest Shackleton

- Be honest but optimistic
- Ensure everyone knows their roles and responsibilities
- Determine progress toward achieving the overall goal
- Look after the welfare and safety of the team
- Build and maintain group cohesion
- Practice risk management

Figure 13.1   The Lessons of Ernest Shackleton.

Be honest but optimistic. Shackleton was honest not only with others but also with himself. Not once during the expedition, did he hide the facts of the situation from his men; doing so would destroy his credibility. He knew that the situation was not good, and he communicated that fact to the men. But he did so in a way that encouraged optimism. Even under some of the most challenging times, he expressed optimism that the situation would improve. True, morale and esprit de corps dwindled, but he always exhibited optimism under the most trying times. The very fact that he continued to try different ways to rescue the men and changing the destination based upon facts and data displayed his optimism that the men would survive. He shared information and communicated his decisions to his men, for example, at all-hands meetings. He knew that if the men lost faith in him and, especially, themselves, despair could result in a disaster.

Ensure everyone knows their roles and responsibilities. Even when hiring for the expedition, Shackleton ensured that everyone knew what their role was and his expectations of them. If they did not perform their roles or failed to meet the expectations, he released and replaced them, as he did in Brazil. After the *Endurance* was no longer serviceable, Shackleton quickly assigned new responsibilities and the corresponding expectations. He assigned men to each of the sledges and communicated his expectations. He also assigned other responsibilities, such as who was responsible for each of the three boats.

Determine progress toward achieving the overall goal. Shackleton and his navigator and captain of the *Endurance*, Frank Worsley, always kept track of their progress. He knew the location of the *Endurance* even to the point of being trapped in a floe. Just as importantly, Shackleton and Worsley knew their location as they were carried by the shifting movement of the floe and as the vessels traversed the sea to South Georgia. Sometimes determining progress was not easy; blizzards, overcasts, and fog sometimes made determining their progress difficult. What was also important was Shackleton used this information to adjust his decision to bring the men to safety. Shackleton never "sugarcoated" the information and communicated the results to his men.

Look after the welfare and safety of the team. Shackleton always considered the welfare and safety of his crew. He did his best to keep his men fed and supplied plenty of water when it was available. Of course, when the expedition failed and turned into a rescue operation, the conditions did not allow the men to maintain a diet to sustain themselves. However, even then he tried to find locations where the men could at least hunt for seals, sea elephants, penguins, and other birds, as well as melt water to quench their thirst. Shackleton was also mindful of the psychological welfare of the men. He recognized that the long hours of darkness could severely impact the mental state of his men. He held celebrations of significant calendar dates, conducted sledge races, kept the men busy hunting seals and other animals, and other activities. He also knew that these activities helped the men relieve their anxiety and nervousness about the situation they had found themselves in. As for safety, he placed a high priority on it. He was constantly fearful that a crack in the ice floe could occur and either separate or kill members of his team; indeed, it did happen a few times, but he managed to deal with the situation with drills and the actual rescue of a man falling into a crack.

Build and maintain group cohesion. From the very beginning of the expedition to its very end, Shackleton knew the importance of teambuilding. He selected men who he thought would be willing to contribute throughout the expedition by sharing in all kinds of tasks, including menial ones, and working with others. When in Brazil, he removed some of the men and replaced them with team players and increased the expedition's expertise. He also was mindful that deteriorating conditions could cause cohesion to disintegrate and jeopardize their survival. When he assigned members of the crew to different tents and sailing in one of the three vessels on the way to South Georgia, he considered not just the personality of the men but also their relationships.

Practice risk management. Shackleton built confidence among the men by always trying to anticipate what risks might exist and determine the response to take. He had many risks, including dwindling food levels, men being separated due to cracks in a floe, despair among the men, not knowing their location, and frostbite. But he was constantly thinking ahead about how to deal with the risks should they become an issue, and they did. While his responses were not always effective, he was willing to try something different. A perfect example was his fear that a crack would separate his crew. He practiced drills to prepare the men to load the sledges and boats and set up regular watches to alert the men.

Final Thoughts

Shackleton knew how to lead, especially in a crisis. He could assess the circumstances, determine the necessary actions, and act. He did so in a way that built confidence among the crew members, not just in him but also within themselves. While it was remarkable in and of itself that he led the men to their rescue, it was also significant that no one died during the expedition, even though many of the men came close to death, including Shackleton. The very act of sailing with five other men to South Georgia on the *James Caird* demonstrated the willingness of the "boss," as the crew called him, to take responsibility for the lives and safety of his men—a true sign of a man who knew everything about leading.

Chapter 14

Conclusion: A Baker's Dozen of Lessons from the Explorers

Most project managers will never experience what the explorers faced during their expeditions. Yet, they can learn from that experience and apply them to their own projects, even programs. Like all projects, their expeditions were based upon a vision of a sponsor, goals were set, resources were allocated and consumed, threats were assessed, stakeholders were determined and analyzed, people were assigned roles and responsibilities recovery actions deployed, and data and information were collected.

Like many projects, too, they faced some of the same challenges that exist on projects today. The vision was vague, the goals were ill-defined, the schedule was unrealistic, not enough resources were available, risks turned into issues and responses were inadequate, sponsors and stakeholders came and went, politics interfered in project execution, not all roles and responsibilities were well-defined, and data and information were unreliable.

Project managers of today learn from the experiences of these explorers. Here are 13 lessons that are applicable to any project (Figure 14.1).

Learn from Experience

Experience is a great learning tool. Ernest Shackleton is a prime example of someone learning from his successes and failures. His previous experiences had a formative

DOI: 10.1201/9781003028734-14

A Baker's Dozen of Lessons from the Explorers

- Learn from experience
- Have a strong sponsor
- Choose your team
- Rely on data and information
- Apply risk management
- Adapt to changing circumstances
- Implement unity of command
- Provide adequate resources
- Identify and understand stakeholders
- Define roles and responsibilities
- Plan, plan, plan
- Be decisive
- Be willing to say no!

Figure 14.1   A Baker's Dozen of Lessons from the Explorers.

impact on how he would handle the potential disaster that confronted him and his crew on his third. It was clear during that expedition that he had reached a level of maturity in his personality that enabled him to save his men from disaster. He was focused but adaptive, bold but not rash, and decisive but not impulsive. His previous experiences laid the groundwork for balancing the need to achieve a goal with the welfare of his men.

Have a Strong Sponsor

Most project managers lack a sponsor as strong as Henry Navigator. The Portuguese prince had a strong vision of what he wanted to see and was intimately involved in the expeditions that he supported, financially and in-kind. He provided the necessary resources and ensured that any lessons were recorded and shared with other explorers. Meriwether Lewis and William Clark had a great sponsor in Thomas Jefferson. Unfortunately, some sponsors are like one that Hernán Cortés with the likes of the governor of Cuba, Diego Velázquez, who eventually changed his support and turned on the conquistador. Fortunate project managers have a sponsor like Henry the Navigator; others have ones like the governor of Cuba. Having a strong, enthusiastic sponsor is a project manager's dream.

Choose Your Team

Many project managers often do not have this luxury, of course. Most project managers must work with people assigned to their project. Roald Amundsen and Ernest Shackleton were two examples, unlike most project managers, of being able to hire their own team; they also had the latitude to dismiss team members who did not perform according to their expectations. Other explorers, however, did not have that opportunity but still managed successful expeditions. George Vancouver and James Cook had the power to inflict discipline, though, which many project managers lack the power to take such drastic action. Still, both captains were able to work with other officers and crew members, some of whom did not like them, to achieve the goals of their expeditions. Most project managers can participate in interview sessions to assess whether a person would be a good fit for their projects.

Rely on Data and Information

Many project managers fall into the trap of hearing what they want to hear and not what they need to hear. In other words, they practice selective hearing. Data and information should be free of bias to determine whether a project is or is not meeting success criteria. Most of the explorers on their expeditions had a good idea of their location using approaches like dead reckoning. Of course, gathering this data and information can be difficult when going through areas that were previously unexplored, such was the case with Vasco da Gama taking an unprecedented approach from the Atlantic to whip around the Cape of Good Hope and Ferdinand Magellan crossing the Pacific Ocean on the way to the Spice Islands. They still looked for celestial and geographic indicators to give them some idea of whether they were reaching their destinations. James Cook managed to explore unknown regions using navigational tools existing at the time. Many projects, at least the exciting ones, are examples of proceeding into the unknown, but still require some idea, based upon data and information, of how well they are reaching their goals.

Apply Risk Management

Not everything is determinable on a project, of course, but project managers should attempt to identify what may happen and prepare a response. Countless risks can arise related to people, processes, data, and systems. Still, good project managers conduct risk management throughout the life cycle of a project. Most of the explorers performed risk management just by the mere act of preparation. James Cook prepared to deal with scurvy by bringing on board extra fruits and vegetables. Vasco da Gama determined he needed extra rigging, sails, and other supplies for the expedition to Calicut. Ernest Shackleton brought extra food for his expedition. Of course, not all risks were identifiable. Shackleton did not anticipate the *Endurance* falling apart and sinking. Cook never anticipated that he would be killed in the Hawaiian Islands. Or Magellan never thought he would be killed in the Philippines.

Adapt to Changing Circumstances

No project proceeds according to plan. Situations arise that require action either to align with a plan or revise the plan to be more realistic. All plans are products of what was known at a specific point in time. Explorers knew this better than anyone, especially when proceeding into unknown territory. Ernest Shackleton was the prime example; he recognized the need to adapt by improvising ways to keep the men alive and revised his destinations based upon the direction of the floe and the strong winds. Meriwether Lewis and William Clark had to adapt to the environment they found themselves. Sometimes they floated down the Missouri, only to encounter falls or river forks, which required altering their plans. Most projects experience problems that require revising revision due to impractical technological approaches or a revision in the schedule or budget.

Implement Unity of Command

The Bible says that no man should serve two masters. Nothing can destroy the unity of command more than the splitting of leadership on a project. It is rare when it works, and it has occasionally as Meriwether Lewis and William Clark demonstrated. But that expedition was the exception rather than the rule. Besides, Lewis had the backing of Jefferson, not Clark; to a large extent, the informal power rested with the former. Vitus Bering being overruled by his sea council resulted in disastrous consequences despite history showing that the Dane was correct. Roald Amundsen knew that dividing leadership roles and responsibilities was a prescription for disaster. One can only imagine what would have been the fate of the crew of the *Endurance* if Shackleton had shared his leadership role and responsibility with another. Too many projects have failed when the project manager's position is split among two or more people and a power struggle arises.

Provide Adequate Resources

Having enough labor and nonlabor resources to support a project is critical to achieving success. Naturally, management will always pressure a project manager to manage a project in a manner that is faster, better, and cheaper. When that philosophy prevails, many projects are doomed to failure right from the start. Jacques Cartier faced this problem during his third expedition to Canada. The colony did not have enough people to defend itself from attack from the Iroquois, and he found he had to return to Saint-Malo. Vitus Bering had too many of the wrong resources, which slowed his progress across Siberia, and he was forced to deal with governors and natives to provide the resources that he needed. Ferdinand Magellan thought he had enough resources to support his trek for two years, only to find he had available only six months of food. Sometimes, even the best planning for resources is just not enough. Ernest Shackleton ensured that his expedition had plenty of resources, but the disaster that occurred resulted in not having enough. The explorer who seemed to have sufficient resources available throughout his expedition was Roald Amundsen, who also set up a queue of caches that helped his team to reach the South Pole and return.

Identify and Understand Stakeholders

Most projects, especially ones impacting medium or large businesses, will involve many stakeholders. These stakeholders can include one or more customers, or they can also impact other people or organizations. Of course, the number one stakeholder should always be the customer. Marco Polo was the premier person who knew the importance of understanding his customer, who was, of course, Kublai Khan and the Mongols. He knew the importance of understanding the needs of the customers better than the other stakeholders surrounding the emperor. But Marco also tried to understand the needs of the other stakeholders within the Mongol Empire, including the Chinese and the Indians. He made every effort to speak their language, understand their customs, and even their religions. The result was that he gained a level of confidence from Khan that few others in the court managed to attain. James Cook, despite the tragedy of his third voyage, and George Vancouver made considerable effort to identify and work with the various native peoples, such as the Hawaiians, they had come in contact with. The relationships with some were not 100 percent perfect, but for the most part, the relationships were good. The biggest error was when an explorer treated all the stakeholders as if they were alike, such as Vasco da Gama and Meriwether Lewis and William Clark, thinking trinkets would meet expectations.

Define Roles and Responsibilities

Well-defined roles and responsibilities are keystones for a successful project. Otherwise, people duplicate tasks, rework is constant, people conflict with one another, the ability to adapt to changing situations is hamstrung, and progress slows. The results are inefficient and ineffective project performance. Roald Amundsen, the ultimate planner, knew the importance of defining roles and responsibilities before embarking on an expedition. Ernest Shackleton knew when the *Endurance* became a sea relic that the situation had changed and quickly reassigned roles and responsibilities, such as making assignments regarding the three vessels, sledges, and routine activities regarding bivouacking and responding to a crack in a floe.

Plan, Plan, Plan

Everyone knows that planning for a project is good project management, but very few people do it well. Most plans are so skeletal they are virtually meaningless and are simply nothing more than a simple checklist. The best explorers were the ones who emphasized the importance of planning and did so upfront. Four explorers stand out as excellent planners, and the results of their expeditions show it. The first is James Cook. He made a special effort to plan all his explorations, involving himself in all the details while providing the freedom to explore. George Vancouver did the same, learning from his teacher, Cook. Meriwether Lewis with the help of President Thomas Jefferson planned the expedition down the Missouri River, determined the necessary provisions, and decided how to interact with Native Americans. Ernest Shackleton was a superb planner despite later facing a disastrous situation. He was on top of all the details required for the expedition, including the route to take. Of course, the premier planner was Roald Amundsen, who planned all aspects of the expedition to the minutest detail.

Be Decisive

Nothing is more agonizing for a team than an indecisive project manager. The team becomes demoralized, and the circumstances requiring a decision worsen. Being indecisive is not the same as being deliberative, which requires defining the problem or issue, looking at the options, and selecting the appropriate action. Under some circumstances, little time is available to be deliberative, such as during a crisis. Magellan was decisive, especially when it came to stopping a mutiny within the ranks or proceeding into unknown territory, such as what is known as Drake Passage today. Hernán Cortés was decisive when he faced an onslaught of Aztecs upon his return to Tenochtitlán after the fiasco created by Captain Pedro de Alvarado. The point is that when serious circumstances arise, effective project managers must be decisive rather than being, as an old saying goes, a deer in headlights. It is not good for the project manager, not for the deer, and not for the team.

Be Willing to Say No!

Too many project managers lack the courage to say no to a superior or a sponsor. Doing so has negative impacts on one's psyche and career. But good project managers know when a project is impossible to complete based upon the parameters dictated to them. Some professional societies agree that a project manager has an ethical responsibility to not accept an impossible project. The explorer Jacques Cartier was one such explorer who, on his final expedition, knew he faced an impossible situation. His commander, Roberval, insisted that Cartier return to reestablish Charlesbourg-Royal. Cartier refused; Roberval eventually found himself having to retreat. Ernest Shackleton knew when he could no longer continue an impossible mission. Granted he had total control of the expedition, but he did have sponsors. Nevertheless, he decided to cancel the trek to the South Pole. In the end, both men made the right decision.

Final Thoughts

Project managers can learn a great deal by studying the experiences of explorers and not just the successful ones. Many other explorers had failed expeditions. John Franklin. Sir Richard Burton. Henry Hudson. These names are just a few of the men whose expeditions ended in failure but provided lessons on what to avoid on a project. Few projects proceed smoothly and most do not, just like expeditions. The key is to learn from one's own experience and that of others.

Glossary

Admiral: an individual who commands a fleet of ships who ranks above a captain; multiple levels of rank exist for admirals.

Astrolabe: an instrument used to calculate latitude, consisting of components to represent the stars in the sky at a specific time and solve astronomical problems.

Barge: a flat-bottom boat used to carry cargo near coastal waters.

Bilge: the lowest, broadest bottom of a vessel.

Bow: the forward section of a vessel.

Brigantine: a vessel with two masts with a square rigging on the foremast; frequently used by brigands.

Cache: a small hidden or protected collection of provisions.

Calving: a piece of ice splits from a glacier or iceberg.

Captain: the title given to the commanding officer of a vessel; the rank just below admiral.

Captain-general: a high-ranking military officer, such as a commander in chief of an army or fleet or both.

Caravel: a ship used for exploration during the middle ages, primarily by the Spanish and Portuguese in the Mediterranean and its colonial adventures in Africa, the Mediterranean, and the New World.

Celestial navigation: a method used by navigators to determine the position of a vessel using the horizon and position of the stars and planets.

Chart: a map of the globe used to navigate waters; useful for identifying obstacles, such as rocks and coral reefs, and depth.

Chronometer: a clock used by navigators to help determine the precise position of a vessel; used to determine longitude.

Collier: a vessel used to carry coal.

Comber: a long, curling wave breaking on a coast.

Commodore: a position below the rank of admiral but above that of a captain; has unique responsibilities while in command of a fleet.

Cooper: the person responsible for the caretaking of a ship's stores and cargo.

Course: the direction of a vessel, such as north or southwest.

Cove: a small inlet or bay with overhanging cliffs protected from winds.

Cutter: a small, fast vessel used to support large vessels or a fleet or perform patrolling.

Dead reckoning: a navigational technique used to determine the position, speed, and course of a vessel based upon its previous locations.

Declination: data on the angular position of a vessel north or south of the equator; the difference between true and magnetic north.

Depot: a place that stores large quantities of provisions, such as supplies and food.

Dhow: a vessel with a mast used for transporting goods throughout the waters of the Middle East and Asia.

Doldrums: the area around the equator whereby the wind is calm, impacting the speed of vessels traversing around the globe.

Easterly: winds blowing from the east.

Eclipse: a celestial body obscuring the light from another celestial body, such as in a lunar or solar eclipse.

Floe: a floating ice sheet.

Flogging: a form of punishment used to discipline soldiers and sailors for significant offenses; often required using cat-o'-nine-tails.

Gale: wind blowing over 34 to 47 knots.

Grog: an alcoholic drink consisting of rum, gin, or brandy watered down; provided to sailors during celebrations or dealing with dangerous situations.

Hummock: a small hill or ridge in an ice pack.

Keelboat: a large flatboat used to carry freight on a river.

Knot: a nautical measurement of speed on a per hour basis; a little over 10 percent of one mile per hour on land.

Lateen: a triangular, oblique sail, as opposed to a square-rigged one, forward or aft on a caravel, enabling maneuverability and speed.

Latitude: the angular distance of a vessel's location, or position, north or south of the equator; determined by observing the position of the north star or the sun.

Lieutenant: the lowest rank of an officer below the commander of a vessel; multiple ranks of lieutenants can exist.

Log: the official record of navigational calculation and events on a ship.

Longboat: a large boat that transports stores to and from a ship; it is carried by a much larger vessel and is armed with gun or canon.

Longitude: the angular distance, east or west, of a vessel relative to the Greenwich Mean Time; location is indicated by drees and minutes.

Magnetic North: the northern location on the earth's surface determined by the needle of a magnetic compass; it is not the same as true north.

Mast: a large vertical spar to hold a sail; one or more masts carried on a sailing vessel.

Master: the officer responsible for the navigation of a vessel; the subordinate to the captain of a vessel.

Master's Mate: assistant to the master during the navigation of a ship.

Midshipman: an apprentice, noncommissioned officer on a vessel, usually under the command of a boatswain; a trainee for becoming a commissioned officer.

Nautical mile: a unit of measurement for distance at sea level; it is approximately 6,076 feet but varies according to latitude.

Navigation: directing and managing a vessel's movement from one location to another across a body of water.

Paiza: a golden tablet issued by Kublai Khan that guarantees a traveler safe passage throughout the empire.

Palanquin: an enclosed carriage resting on two poles supported by four or more men to carry an individual.

Pemmican: a dried mixture of fat, meat, and fruit or vegetables; a frequent food source for men and animals exploring the Arctic and Antarctica.

Pirogue: a medium-sized, flat-bottom boat used to transport cargo in backwater areas and rivers; it requires the use of oarsmen and a pilot.

Port: the left side of a vessel.

Post-captain: an officer in the British navy commanding a warship; a commander.

Quadrant: four sections of a magnetic compass card; each quadrant equals 90 degrees.

Sastrugi: ridges on a surface of hard snow, caused by severe winds.

Sault: rapids in a river.

Scurvy: a disease caused by a lack of Vitamin C, caused mainly by a diet void of fruits and vegetables; it can result in severe illness and even death.

Sledge: a vehicle on runners pulled by animals, sometimes humans, carrying supplies, provisions, etc. over snow and ice.

Spit: low level of sediment, such as a shoal, accumulating in a zigzag pattern off a beach.

Squall: a sudden strong wind or storm due to the passage of climatic depression.

Starboard: the right side of a vessel.

Stern: the rear section of a vessel; also known as the aft.

Tacking: the zigzagging or crossing movement of a vessel into the wind.

Trade Winds: steady winds blowing 30 degrees north or south of the equator; the winds move northeast in the Northern Hemisphere and southeast in the Southern Hemisphere.

True North: the direction of the North Pole from any position of a vessel; the position of the North Pole is reflected on a navigation map.

Windward: the downwind side of a vessel used for steering away from obstacles; the side of the vessel toward the wind.

Zamorin: a Hindu monarch of the Kingdom of Calicut.

About the Author

Ralph Kliem, PMP (Project Management Professional) and CBCP (Certified Business Continuity Professional), is founder and president of LeanPM, LLC, and has over 30 years of combined experience in the private and public sectors as a project manager and internal auditor. He holds an M.A. in political science; is a member of social, history, and political science honor societies; a former legislative intern; and an artillery officer. He retired from the Boeing Company where he conducted enterprise risk assessments and audits of its political action committee, evaluated lobbying activities, managed the development of business continuity plans for its major airplane programs, and taught professional seminars and workshops on project and program management throughout the corporation and its clients, such as Ford, General Motors, Department of Defense, Internal Revenue Service, and other corporations and public institutions. He has authored more than 15 books with major publishers and over 300 articles for leading business and information technology magazines.

He is a frequent speaker at Project Management Institute chapters and other events. He has developed and delivered project management courses for Cascadia Community College and Bellevue College. He also delivers seminars and workshops for corporate clients through Key Consulting, Inc. and the Business Productivity Center, Inc. throughout the United States, Canada, and the Caribbean. He was an instructor at City University of Seattle and a former adjunct faculty member with Seattle Pacific University.

His book publications include:

- *Business Continuity Planning* (CRC Press., ISBN: 978-1-4822-5178-4)
- *Creative, Efficient, and Effective Project Management* (Auerbach, ISBN: 9781466576926)
- *Effective Communications for Project Management* (Auerbach, ISBN: 978-1-4200-6246-5)
- *Ethics and Project Management* (Auerbach, ISBN: 978–1439852613)
- *Leading High Performance Projects* (J. Ross Publishing, ISBN: 1–932159–10-X)
- *Managing Lean Projects* (CRC Press, ISBN: 978-1-4822-5182-1)
- *Managing Projects in Trouble* (Auerbach, ISBN: 978-1-4398-5246-0)
- *Tools and Tips for Today's Project Manager* (Project Management Institute, ISBN 1-880410-61-3)

Bibliography

Alexander, Caroline. 1998. *The Endurance*. Thorndike, ME: G. K. Hall & Co.

Allen, John Logan. 1975. *Lewis and Clark and the Image of the American Northwest*. New York: Dover Publications, Inc.

Ambrose, Stephen E. 1997. *Undaunted Courage*. New York: Simon and Schuster.

Anderson, Bern. 1960. *The Life and Voyages of Captain George Vancouver*. Seattle, WA: University of Washington Press.

Aughton, Peter. 2007. *The Fatal Voyage*. New York: Tauris Parke Paperbacks.

Bart, Sheldon. 2013. *Race to the Top of the World*. Washington, DC: Regnery Publishing, Inc.

Batman, Richard. 2001. *The Outer Coast*. Edison, NJ: Castle Books.

Bergon, Frank, ed. 1989. *The Journals of Lewis and Clark*. New York: Penguin Books.

Bergreen, Laurence. 2003. *Over the Edge of the World*. New York: William Morrow.

Bergreen, Laurence. 2007. *Marco Polo*. New York: Alfred A. Knopf.

Bergreen, Laurence. 2011. *Columbus*. New York: Viking.

Bernstein, Peter L. 2000. *The Power of Gold*. New York: John Wiley & Sons, Inc.

Berton, Pierre. 1988. *The Arctic Grail*. Toronto, Canada: Anchor Canada.

Blake, E. Vale. 2013. *Journey to the Arctic*. New York: Skyhorse Publishing.

Blumenthal, Richard W. 2007. *With Vancouver in Inland Washington Waters*. Jefferson, NC: McFarland & Company, Inc.

Blumenthal, Richard W. 2014. *British Columbia Waters*. Bellevue, WA: Inland Publishing Co.

Bohlander, Ricard E., ed. 1992. *World of Explorers and Discoverers*. New York: MacMillan Publishing Company.

Boorstin, Daniel J. 1985. *The Discoverers*. New York: Vintage Books.

Brinkbaumer, Klaus and Hoges, Clemens. 2006. *The Voyage of the Vizcaina*. Orlando: Harcourt, Inc.

Brodie, Fawn M. 1967. *The Devil Drives*. New York: William Norton and Company, Inc.

Camusso, Lorenzo. 1991. *The Voyages of Columbus 1492–1504*. New York: Dorset Press.

Cantor, Norman F., ed. 1999. *The Encyclopedia of the Middle Ages*. New York: Viking Penguin.

Collingridge, Vanessa. 2002. *Captain Cook*. Guilford, CT: The Lyons Press.

Collis, Maurice. 1955. *Cortes and Montezuma*. New York: Harcourt, Brace, and Company.

Cook, James. 1999. *The Voyages of Captain Cook*. Hertfordshire: Wordsworth Editions Limited.

Cortes, Hernando. 1998. *Five Letters from Mexico*. Princeton: Collectors Reprints, Inc.

Cox, Lynne. 2011. *South with the Sun*. Boston: Mariner Books.

Crutchfield, James A. 1999. *It Happened in Washington*. Guilford, CT: The Globe Pequot Press.

Cutright, Paul R. 2003. *Lewis and Clark*. Lincoln, NB: University of Nebraska Press.

de Fuentes, Patricia. 1993. *The Conquistadors*. Norman, OK: University of Oklahoma Press.

D'Epiro, Peter and Pinkowish, Mary Desmond. 2001. *Sprezzatura*. New York: Anchor Books.

Desowitz, Roberts. 1997. *Who Gave Pinta to the Santa Maria?* New York: W. W. Norton & Company.

De Voto, Bernard, ed. 1997. *The Journals of Lewis and Clark*. Boston: Houghton Mifflin Company.

Diaz, Bernal. 1963. *The Conquest of New Spain*. London: Penguin Books.

Dietrich, William. 1995. *Northwest Passage*. New York: Simon and Schuster.

Dor-Ner, Zevi. 1991. *Columbus and the Age of Discovery*. New York: William Morrow and Company, Inc.

Dugard, Martin. 2001. *Farther Than Any Man*. New York: Washington Square Press.

Dugard, Martin. 2006. *The Last Voyage of Columbus*. New York: Little, Brown, and Company.

Dugard, Martin. 2014. *The Explorers*. New York: Simon and Schuster.

Edmonds, Jane, ed. 1997. *Atlas of Exploration*. New York: Oxford University Press.

Fernandez-Armesto, Felipe. 2006. *Pathfinders*. New York: W. W. Norton and Company.

Ficken, Robert E. and LeWarne, Charles P. 1989. *Washington*. Seattle, WA: University of Washington Press.

Fifer, Barbara and Soderberg, Vicky. 2001. *Along the Trailer with Lewis and Clark*. 2nd ed. Helena, MT: Farcountry Press.

Fleming, Fergur. 2001. *Ninety Degrees North*. New York: Grove Press.

Freuchen, Peter. 1958. *Book of the Seven Seas*. London: Jarrold & Sons, Ltd.

Fried, Johannes. Trans. by Peter Lewis. 2015. *The Middle Ages*. Cambridge, MA: Belknap Press.

Frost, Orcutt. 2003. *Bering*. New Haven, CT: Yale University Press.

Fusion, Robert H. 1992. *The Log of Christopher Columbus*. Camden, ME: International Marine Publishing.

Gaudalupi, Gianni and Shugar, Antony. 2001. *Latitude Zero*. New York: Carroll & Graf Publishers.

Gilman, Carolyn. 2003. *Lewis and Clark Across the Divide*. St. Louis: Smithsonian Books.

Gooley, Tristian. 2011. *The Natural Navigator*. New York: The Experiment.

Granberg, W. J. 1960. *Voyage into Darkness*. New York: E. P. Dutton and Company, Inc.

Gulick, Bill. 1996. *A Traveler's History of Washington*. Caldwell, ID: The Caxton Printers, Ltd.

Gurney, Alan. 1998. *Below the Convergence*. New York: Penguin Books.

Hall, W. B. 1972. *The Romance of Navigation*. New York: Benjamin Blom, Inc.

Halsey, Cheryll. 2006. *Lewis and Clark Across the Northwest*. Blaine, WA: Hancock House Publishers.

Hanbury-Tenison, Robin. 1993. *The Oxford Book of Exploration*. Oxford: Oxford University Press.

Hanbury-Tenison, Robin. 2010. *The Great Explorers*. 2nd ed. London: Thames and Hudson, Ltd.

Hayes, Derek. 2003. *Historical Atlas of the Arctic*. Seattle, WA: University of Washington Press.

Horwitz, Tony. 2002. *Blue Latitudes*. New York: Henry Holt and Company.

Hough, Richard. 1997. *Captain James Cook*. New York: W. W. Norton and Company.

Humble, Richard. 1979. *The Explorers*. Alexandria, VA: Time-Life Books.

Huntford, Roland. 1985. *Shackleton*. New York: Carroll & Graf Publishers, Inc.

Huntford, Roland. 1999. *The Last Place on Earth*. New York: Modern Library.

Innes, Hammond. 1969. *The Conquistadors*. New York: Alfred A. Knopf.

Jeal, Tim. 2011. *Explorers of the Nile*. New Haven, CT: Yale University Press.

Jeans, Peter D. 2004. *Ship to Shore*. Camden, ME: McGraw-Hill.

Jones, Landon Y., ed. 2002. *The Essential Lewis and Clark*. New York: Ecco.

Josephy Jr., Alvin M., ed. 2006. *Lewis and Clark Through Indian Eyes*. New York: Alfred A. Knopf.

Keay, John, ed. 1993. *The Permanent Book of Exploration*. New York: Carroll & Graf Publishers, Inc.

Kelsey, Harry. 2016. *The First Circumnavigators*. New Haven: Yale University Press.

Kemp, Peter, ed. 1994. *The Oxford Companion to Ships and the Sea*. Oxford: Oxford University Press.

Kennedy, Gavin. 1978. *The Death of Captain Cook*. London: Duckworth.

Kirkpatrick, F. A. 1967. *The Spanish Conquistadors*. Cleveland, OH: Meridian Books.

Kjellstrom, Bjorn. 1976. *Be Expert with Map and Compass*. New York: Charles Scribner's Sons.

Krondl, Michael. 2007. *The Taste of Conquest*. New York: Ballantine Books.

Lansing, Alfred. 1999. *Endurance*. 7th ed. New York: Carroll and Graf Publishers.

Lavender, David. 1988. *The Way to the Western Sea*. New York: Anchor Books.

Lavery, Brian. 2013. *The Conquest of the Ocean*. New York: DK Books.

Lester, Toby. 2010. *The Fourth Part of the World*. New York: Free Press.

Levinson, Nancy Smiler. 2001. *Magellan and the First Voyage Around the World*. New York: Clarion Books.

Levy, Buddy. 2009. *Conquistador*. New York: Bantam Books.

Lewis, Jon E., ed. 1998. *The Mammoth Book of Eye-Witness History*. New York: Carroll & Graf Publishers, Inc.

Liulevicius, Gabriel. 2015. *History's Greatest Voyages of Exploration Course Guide Book*. Chantilly, WA: The Great Courses.

Lopez de Goma, Francisco. 1964. *Cortes*. Berkeley, CA: University of California Press.

McGougan, Ken. 2008. *Race to the Polar Sea*. Berkeley: Counterpoint.

Miller, Gordon. 2011. *Voyages to the New World and Beyond*. Seattle, WA: University of Washington Press.

Millward, James. 2013. *The Silkroad*. Oxford: Oxford University Press.

Mixter, George W. 1979. *Primer of Navigation*. New York: Van Nostrand Reinhold Company.

Moody, Alton B. 1980. *Navigation Afloat*. New York: Van Nostrand Reinhold Company.

Morgan, Murray. 1979. *Puget's Sound*. Seattle, WA: University of Washington Press.

Morison, Samuel Eliot. 1971. *The European Discovery of America*. New York: Oxford University Press.

Morison, Samuel Eliot. 1991. *Christopher Columbus*. Greenwich, CT: Dorset Press.

Morrell, Margot and Capparell, Stephanie. 2002. *Shackleton's Way*. New York: Penguin Books.

Newman, James L. 2010. *Paths without Glory*. Washington, DC: Potomac Books, Inc.

Polo, Marco. 1997. *The Travels of Marco Polo*. Hertfordshire: Wordsworth Editions, Limited.

Prescott, William H. 2000. *History of the Conquest of Mexico and History of the Conquest of Peru*. New York: Cooper Square Press.

Preston, Diana. 1998. *A First Rate Tragedy*. Boston: Mariner Books.

Price, A. Grenfell, ed. 1971. *The Explorations of James Cook*. New York: Dover Publications.

Quinn, David B., ed. 1971. *North American Discovery*. New York: Harper and Row, Publishers.

Rice, Edward. 1990. *Captain Sir Francis Burton*. New York: Charles Scribner's Sons.

Roberts, J. M. 2002. *The New Penguin History of the World*. London: Penguin Books.

Robson, Hohn. 2004. *The Captain Cook Encyclopaedia*. London: Chatham Publishing.

Rogers, John G. 1985. *Origins of Sea Terms*. Boston: The American maritime Library.

Ronda, James P. 1984. *Lewis and Clark among the Indians*. Lincoln, NB: University of Nebraska Press.

Russell, Peter. 2000. *Prince Henry the Navigator*. New Haven, CT: Yale Nota Bene.

Sahlins, Marshall. 1995. *How Natives Think*. Chicago: The University of Chicago Press.

Sale, Kirkpatrick. 1991. *The Conquest of Paradise*. New York: Plume.

Sale, Roger. 1978. *Seattle*. Seattle, WA: University of Washington Press.

Salmond, Anne. 2003. *The Trial of the Cannibal Dog*. New Haven, CT: Yale University Press.

Sansevere-Dreher, Diane. 2015. *Explorer's Who Got Lost*. New York: Tor Books.

Sass, Erik and Wiegand, Steve. 2008. *History of the World*. New York: Harper Collins.

Schwantes, Carlos Arnaldo. 1996. *The Pacific Northwest*. Lincoln, NB: University of Nebraska Press.

Scott, R. F. 2011. *Scott's Last Expedition*. Hertfordshire: Wordsworth Editions Limited.

Shackleton, Ernest. 1998. *South*. New York: Carroll & Graf.

Speck, Gordon. 1954. *Northwest Explorations*. Portland, OR: Binfords and Mort.

Speke, John H. 2015. *The Source of the Nile*. Gloucestershire: Amberley.

Steller, Georg Wilhelm. 1988. *Journal of a Voyage with Bering 1741–1742*. Stanford, CA: Stanford University Press.

Thomas, Hugh. 1993. *Conquest*. New York: Touchstone.

Thomas, Hugh. 2003. *Rivers of Gold*. New York: Random House.

Thomas, Nicolas. 2003. *Cook*. New York: Walker & Company.

Townsend, Richard F. 1993. *The Aztecs*. New York: Thames and Hudson.

Vaugh, Thomas. 1974. *Captain Cook, R. N.* Portland, OR: Oregon Historical Society.

Viola, Herman J. and Margolis, Carolyn, eds. 1985. *Magnificent Voyagers*. Washington, DC: Smithsonian Institution.

Whall, W. B. 1972. *The Romance of Navigation*. New York: Benjamin Blom, Inc.

Whitebrook, Robert B. 1959. *Coastal Exploration of Washington*. Palo Alto, CA: Pacific Books.

Wilcox, Desmond. 1977. *Ten Who Dared*. Boston: Little, Brown, and Company.

Wilford, John Noble. 2000. *The Mapmakers*. New York: Vintage Books.

Williams, Glyn. 2002. *Voyages of Delusion*. Hammersmith: Harper Collins, Publishers.

Wood, Michael. 2000. *Conquistadors*. Berkeley, CA: University of California Press.

Worsley, F. A. 1977. *Shackleton's Boat Journey*. New York: W. W. Norton & Company, Inc.

Worsley, F. A. 1999. *Endurance*. New York: W. W. Norton & Company.

Zug, James, ed. 2005. *The Last Voyage of Captain Cook*. Washington, DC: National Geographic Society.

Zweig, Stefan. 1938. *The Story of Magellan*. New York: The Viking Press.

Index

Note: Page numbers in *italic* indicate a figure on the corresponding page.

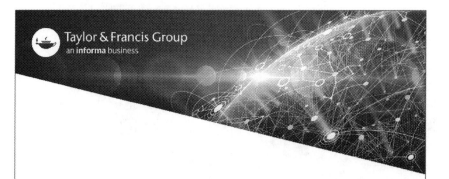

Printed in the United States
by Baker & Taylor Publisher Services